# THE CRUSADER

# THE CRUSADER

*How Modi Won 2019 Elections*

RANDEEP SISODIA

Srishti
PUBLISHERS & DISTRIBUTORS

**Srishti Publishers & Distributors**
A unit of AJR Publishing LLP
212A, Peacock Lane
Shahpur Jat, New Delhi – 110 049
editorial@srishtipublishers.com

First published by
Srishti Publishers & Distributors in 2021



10 9 8 7 6 5 4 3 2 1

This is a work of non-fiction based on the author's observation and understanding of Indian polity. This publication is meant as a source of information for the reader, but not as a replacement for direct expert assistance. While due care has been taken at press time to ensure no party/ institution/ individual is disrespected or hurt through the narrative, any such instances shall be rectified in subsequent prints after being brought to notice.



Printed and bound in India

*This book is dedicated to my parents,*
*Suman and Ranbir,*
*whose love, affection and blessings*
*are the reasons for my existence.*

# Contents

# Acknowledgements

I will forever be indebted to my family, my parents, my late grandparents and relations for having instilled in me a sense of responsibility and pride for the nation and for having exposed me to a diverse range of thoughts, especially on Indian polity and religion during my normative years.

Writing a book requires single-minded focus and stretched periods of solitude. Special thanks to my wife Menka for her unflinching support, understanding and care.

I learnt the science of leadership during my management studies, but most importantly, I learnt the art of leadership through its practice during my long stint in the corporate world. I learnt the importance of having a worldview and expressing it fearlessly. These learnings were key enablers in penning this book. I thank all my teachers and colleagues from the corporate world who have touched my life and interacted with me, thereby enriching me.

While writing is a solitary practise, presenting it to the world is a team sport. Many thanks to Arup Bose, Stuti and the team at Srishti Publishers & Distributors for warmly welcoming me and for their partnership, advise, support and help in bringing this book to life in the most appropriate way.

Above all, I want to thank God for giving me the opportunity, strength, motivation and ability to offer this book to you, my esteemed readers!

# Preface

## *Darr Lagta Hai!*

***Hoshiarpur, Punjab***
***During Emergency days***

Scores of RSS members went to prison after the organisation was banned, while quite a few were forced to go into hiding to avoid arrest. At that time, when no lawyer was ready to take up the cases of these hapless people, my father took up the challenge and fought for them in court. We experienced, first hand, how people had to roam around in disguise and sneak out from the back doors of houses to save themselves from being arrested. Yet, it never once came to our mind – "*Darr lagta hai.*" (I am scared.)

On a fateful night during the dark days of terrorism in Punjab, a direct result of politics meddling in religion, a mob of bloodthirsty fanatics attacked a house a few hundred metres away from ours, and tried to put it on fire. The next night and for a few nights thereafter, my grandparents, my parents, my brother and I spent the night in one room. Before sleeping, my father would draw out his double barrel gun from the closet and load it with two bullets. The gun would then rest against the wall, at arms-length next to his pillow, and only then we went to sleep. Earlier, my brother and I eagerly waited for the once-a-year ritual when my father pulled out his gun for polishing. We would marvel at the site of that beauty. However, this time around, we were finding it repulsive.

Hoshiarpur is a small, sleepy, nondescript town that, just like any other village, town or city in Punjab, was making headlines, for all the wrong reasons, in national newspapers during the peak of terrorism days. Those days when the bread earner of the family went out to work, the family wasn't sure of his safe return in the evening.

One such evening, a neighbour came running to our house and mentioned that there had been a blast in the courts. We panicked, as my father was in court at that time. I immediately grabbed my bicycle and rushed out of the house towards the court. One person had died and many were injured in that blast. We were lucky that my father was safe.

Once, coming back from Chandigarh in a Punjab roadways bus, passing through the hinterland during late evening, our bus suddenly came to a halt. I could see a lot of people outside, along with a few police vehicles. A couple of police officers walked in, quickly scanned the bus and signalled the driver to move on. Later we found out that a few minutes before us, another Punjab roadways bus was taken off track forcefully by the terrorists, who then segregated people and killed them. We kept having these close shaves, but never once did the expression "Darr lagta hai" occurred to us. Of course, there was fear, but we never thought that it was scary to live in this country. There were many people worse off than us, who lost loved ones, and yet, we never heard that sentiment.

Back then too, every community suffered – many Sikhs who opposed terrorists lost their lives, and there were reports of fake encounters, of innocents being booked because of mistaken identities, of families being wrongly harassed even when they were genuinely unaware that their young ones had joined the terrorists. There was terror all around and every law-abiding citizen was feeling the heat. But despite all that, we never ever heard that sentiment.

Punjab being a prosperous state, generally people had the maturity to understand the politics and futility behind all the violence. Since they understood the real game behind all this, the people-to-people relations continued to be normal. In fact, the tough times strengthened the bonds even further. Celebrities and influential people cut across caste and community to promote sanity, goodwill and appealled for calm while condemning the violent acts of the misguided. That also acted as a balm on commoners, and generally, better sense prevailed.

Hence, when one hears some celebrities, celebrated artists and intellectuals today, comfortably ensconced in their plush air-conditioned and protected environments, having never had to face terror or state oppression, express that sentiment, "Darr lagta hai", one can't help but wonder the hypocrisy of it all. And when you realise that such statements invariably are made just when an election season is about to begin, you realise the politics of it all!

It is as if these privileged elites, have worn the boxing gloves but refuse to enter the ring. They punch from outside the ring. They know very well that the boxer inside will not hit them for fear of disqualification. In all fairness, a few of these celebrities have entered the ring, and have been ready to take the blows.

Kudos to them! However, they soon realised that they were completely irrelevant; they were like an amateur feather weight category boxer taking on a veteran heavyweight professional. And the professional, forget about hitting, did not even pay any attention to them. As they say, there is a difference between 'reel' life and 'real' life. Perhaps, what they really are scared of is entering the ring in real life.

At another level, irrespective of whatever the reason, one would have to term it as highly irresponsible and perhaps even mischievous behaviour. In a country with widespread illiteracy and poverty that leads to insecurity and fear, such statements by the elite and influential class does tantamount to fear mongering among the masses. It is in this context that one feels that being a celebrity, whose words have immense influencing power, requires him or her to be a lot more responsible than any other citizen. They should measure their words twice before they speak, especially on sensitive subjects. They should pause and think, who is it really going to benefit? And more importantly, is it really going to help the cause of people who actually are oppressed? It is good to know your rights, but it is an absolute essential to understand your responsibilities.

The fundamental point here is that a celebrity is a celebrity. He has no religion. People have loved him irrespective of his religion and people from all religions have admired him. It is insincere of him to play the religion card. He should rather be assuring people than fear-mongering. Or else, he should jump into the real world of politics and transparently declare which side is he on.

Now for those in positions of authority, who are hell bent on sending everyone who opposes them to Pakistan, perhaps they have a wrong notion that they work for Pakistan Embassy, which is the only authority to send people to Pakistan. On a serious note, if the celebrities and celebrated folk need to think twice before they speak, the lawmakers and politicians need to think at least four times before they utter something. By just shooting from their mouth, they are doing a huge disservice to the government, which is working on solving legacy problems besetting this country since decades.

I also dedicate this book to all those who remain committed and dedicated to this nation called India. Especially those who face hardships, undergo strife, harassment, even oppression and yet continue to put faith and trust in this country. This 'silent aspirational India', unmindful of the fierce and motivated propaganda, continues its daily grind in a lawful and orderly way.

The real purpose of this book is to look beyond the debates on 'Darr Lagta Hai', 'intolerance' and issues that only view things from a Hindu-Muslim binary. These are all illusions conjured up by vested interests, and instead, the book attempts to raise the level of political discourse, reminding ourselves of the real purpose of polity and the criticality of winning the trust of people. A key purpose of the book is to search for the soul of India and rediscover the idea of India, the idea that is the uniting factor in our unity in diversity.

Finally, since we talked of the dark days of Punjab, it will only be apt to end this section with a tribute to the exuberant Punjabi spirit, of making light of the most trying situations, and what better than a hilarious anecdote to highlight that. During those strife-torn days in Punjab, the media would be full of news on violent incidents, and as is its wont, often exaggerate it beyond proportions. While people within Punjab generally went along with their day-to-day lives normally, barring the fear factor, many people residing outside of Punjab would generally develop the impression as if it was a war-ravaged state.

Therefore, in that backdrop, once a Punjabi went to a relative's place in Delhi. The relative, empathetic towards him says, "It must be such a terrible situation for you back there. If not seeing incidents, you surely must be hearing gun shots often enough".

The Punjabi promptly responded, "Often enough? Well, when we walk on the streets, we are literally ducking and dodging all the time, saving ourselves from the bullets being fired all around us".

No matter how difficult a situation one may be in, one must always try to see the lighter side of things. It makes life a lot easier.

# Part I
# *Challenging the Order*

# 1
# The Khan Market Gang (KMG)

On 15 August 1947, as India attained freedom at the stroke of the midnight hour, monarchy was back, and how! Under the garb of democracy.

By 1946, it was clear that the British would abrogate power and since Congress was the only political party in existence, it was a foregone conclusion that the President of the Congress Party would be the first Prime Minister of India. For the President post of the party, 12 out of 15 Congress state committees voted for Vallabh Bhai Patel, and none voted for Jawaharlal Nehru. Yet, Bapu (Mahatma Gandhi) vetoed the people's voice and appointed Nehru as the President, who then, by virtue of that position, went on to become the first Prime Minister of India. Ironically, the first Prime Minister of an independent democratic India was 'selected' and not 'elected'.

28 December 1885: The Indian National Congress was founded at the initiative of a retired British civil services officer, Allan Octavian Hume, with a goal to provide greater share in British Raj for educated Indians and to create a platform for dialogue between them and the Raj. Hence, the Congress party

was founded under the aegis of the monarchy with a view to fulfil elite India's ambitions. It was an insincere and dishonest ploy by the British to keep the educated and politically aware Indians engaged, so they did not embark on a rebellious route. The formation of the party was such that the reins always remained with the British monarchy.

Men like Bal Gangadhar Tilak, one of the two tallest leaders of the Congress, pushed the envelope and demanded *purna swaraj* or self-rule. However, for this temerity, he was sent to prison. The other stalwart of Congress, Gopal Krishna Gokhale, had accepted to work under the British dominion. However, his attempts to work for the improvement of education and health of the Indian lot failed to move the British. In fact, unknowingly, he was used by the British to push their own agendas. In hindsight, it was clear the British saw Congress as a key instrument to further tighten their grip on India.

It was only after Bapu (Mahatma Gandhi) joined the Congress and worked on issues that affected the ordinary and poor that it became a mass movement, which awakened and united a disparate swathe of Indian people. Bapu channelized that unity against the might of the British Raj, which established him as a numero uno of the Congress. Indeed, there came a time when Bapu, forget being taller than any other leader within the party, was taller than Congress itself. People followed Bapu, not Congress. He was the undisputed and supreme leader of the Congress party, irrespective of whosoever was the head of the Congress.

In this way, the reins of the Congress party had passed on from the British to Bapu. In 1929, Nehru was selected to be the President of the party. Motilal Nehru, who was then presiding as the Congress President, had put in a strong recommendation in his son's favour to Bapu. He had a strong bias for Nehru anyway. In another instance in 1939, Subhash Chandra Bose was elected as the Congress President, but he resigned when Bapu expressed his open displeasure on Bose's election. Bose resigned, as he did not want to break the party. Bapu's decision to veto Congress's vote for Patel and choosing Nehru to be the first Prime Minister has been a subject of many debates and would continue to be a hotly contested subject in future too.

It did not surprise people when the vote of Congressmen was vetoed by Bapu. Congress owed its existence in a large measure to Bapu. He had given them a real purpose, showed them the way, taught them how to walk and guided them all through the way. Had it not been for him, it was quite probable that Congress would have disintegrated and become irrelevant. Congressmen understood that and quietly bowed to his will. It can be reasonably assumed that irrespective of the apparent democratic processes institutionalised on paper within Congress, for all practical purposes, Bapu's writ run large. If he did not agree with the vote, the Congressmen would obediently come around and accept his decision. However, under Bapu, it has to be said that Congress party was a benevolent monarchy, fighting for the cause of the poor and dispossessed.

Bapu had his blind spots. After all, we forget that he was a human too and liable to make mistakes. Many thought that Nehru was not worthy enough to be the premier of the country, but then Bapu had proclaimed Nehru as his heir apparent, and hence he was entitled. In his book, *India from Curzon to Nehru and After*, the author Durga Das writes, "I mentioned Rajendra Prasad's (who went on to become the first President of India) lament expressed to me that Gandhi had once again sacrificed his trusted lieutenant (Patel) for the sake of the glamorous Nehru and the fear that Nehru would follow British ways." There are many other accounts of other tall Congress leaders of that time expressing similar sentiments.

Thus, over the years, the reins of the party and the country went, for all practical purposes, from a mighty imperialist to a deserving and a benevolent monarch who lived like a fakir, and finally to the one who was an undeserving entitled dynast.

From then on, as time went by, the Congress party would go on to assume the traits of Dynastic monarchy. The Nehru clan would eventually adopt Bapu's surname, Gandhi, and the gullible citizenry of India would get deceived, thinking the Nehru clan to be the rightful owners of Bapu's legacy. Today, there is no bigger proof of Congress being a monarchy than the Congressmen themselves, who proudly proclaim that the Congress exists only because of the Nehru-Gandhi dynasty and if the dynasty were not at the helm, it would disintegrate. It is ironic that despite giving so many sacrifices in the hard-fought independence struggle against a monarchy, Indians were now voting for a monarchy!

The most essential characteristic in a monarchic structure is the establishment of *darbaris* or courtiers. It needs a set of intellectuals who are not just committed to the monarch, but also to the perpetuation of his clan, the dynasty. These darbaris don't just help run day-to-day affairs of the monarch, but their prime goal is to ensure that his dynasty sustains for generations. These loyal darbaris are the eyes, the ears and most importantly, the brains behind the dynasty. This was, perhaps, the genesis of the Khan Market Gang (KMG). As the power at the top shifted from one generation to other, so did the modern day darbaris, the 'KMG', who supposedly kept on transferring its reins from one generation of loyalists to the other, assuming a dynastic character of its own, with each generation pledging its allegiance to the monarch's dynasty.

Khan Market in Delhi is an upmarket place for elites, close to the seat of power, surrounded by exquisite bungalows and plush apartments where the who's who live. It perhaps is one of the most expensive locations in India, housing top luxury brands and expensive restaurants serving all kinds of cuisines from across the globe. The place is supposed to be frequently visited by these darbaris, and it is considered that it is here that they would gossip, plot, connive on issues of national importance; manufacture myths and create imaginary controversies – hence the term Khan Market Gang. This devious entity consists of the most brilliant of influencers of their times – bureaucrats, journalists, left intellectuals, lawyers, academics, lobbyists, fixers, etc.

The KMG continued to perpetuate the imperialistic doctrine, which ascribed to a view that Indians were losers and hence needed to be governed by western educated intellectuals. Over a period of time, especially 1970s onwards, they became the symbol of India's crony socialism. They would exploit their access to power and dubious networks to influence quotas, licenses, appointments and awards. In addition to that, since it was well known that this group also controlled the media (it was easier back then as electronic media was state controlled and the print media, especially English, was dominated by left leaning intellectuals), it continued its domination on the narrative of the idea of India. This idea of India suited the Nehru dynasty, which was in power for more than fifty years since 1947 and hence this cabal gained from strength to strength.

For any monarchy, it is critical to control the national narrative in favour of its dynasty. It needs to project it in the most favourable light and position it as one of the most powerful ever in the history of its kingdom. It requires an extremely effective propaganda machine and that gave birth to Lutyen's media. KMG would have realised the importance of media pretty early, and hence, apparently co-opted senior journalists and influential media professionals. Largesse was showered on them to keep them in good humour and on the dynasty's side. Quite a few of them were given residences near the seat of power, in Lutyen's Delhi, hence the term Lutyen's media.

Lutyen's media, in partnership with KMG, played a critical role in the sustenance and indeed the perpetuation of the dynasty by spinning an idea of India, which had its root only in the twentieth-century Independence struggle, as nothing worthwhile happened before that. In fact, the impression created was that India as a nation did not exist before that. For the continuation of the dynasty, it was necessary to play down the rich heritage of India and somehow position the great awakening of the nation in line with the emergence of the Nehru dynasty. The common citizenry was, pounded by this idea of India so heavily that they were lulled into believing in it for a length of time.

It was perhaps this illusion that Modi was hell bent on breaking as he assumed the Prime Minister's office in May 2014. As Modi ascended the political throne of India, he sidelined this gang. The access to the corridors of power was denied and the entitlements and privileges snatched away. All middlemen and fixers were banned from entering North and South block. The KMG as well as the Lutyen's media were pushed to irrelevance.

The dynastic order in peril, the KMG decided to hit back, and thus were planted the seeds for 'defeat Modi plan – 2019'.

Given Modi's unparalleled stature and popularity, the plan was that instead of getting into a direct fight at a national level in 2019 elections, to fight 543 local battles at each of the 543 constituencies, putting one opposition candidate against Bharatiya Janta Party's (BJP)/NDA's candidate per constituency, fighting only on local issues. To bolster this plan, it was suggested that the opposition should go into the general elections without a leader, to avoid a direct presidential fight with Modi.

The premise used was spotless. After all, as mentioned earlier, these were sharp minds. In 2014, Modi successfully positioned himself as a protagonist who was challenging the corrupt and rotting system of the Delhi durbar. He was the challenger, the white knight in shining armour, who single-handedly demolished the Delhi sultanate.

In 2019, the tables were going to turn. It was for Modi now to defend his Delhi citadel. Since as per the KMG plan, the joint opposition would not directly attack Delhi but open up 543 different fronts simultaneously, it would make it physically impossible for Modi to defend each constituency effectively, in order to save the Delhi throne.

At the time this plan was crafted, it would have been a very difficult to pick a hole in it. It seemed that the KMG had created a perfect plan. Key elements of this plan brought back memories of a doctrine against India, then much publicised, propounded by one of its neighbouring adversary, Pakistan.

In 1965, at UN Security council, Zulfikar Ali Bhutto, the then Foreign Minister of Pakistan, in his eloquent and impassioned speech declared a thousand-year war against India, painting India as an aggressive monster who was out there to eliminate Pakistan from the face of this earth. Subsequently, Zia-ul-Haq, the Pak Army Chief, operationalised this declaration by infiltrating trained terrorists into India to cause bloodshed and unrest, through a long and porous border on the west of India as well as from Nepal and Bangladesh. Rather than directly attacking India, this covert and low intensity warfare doctrine, where Pakistan would infiltrate individual mercenaries into India from various points to create mayhem and destruction in a thousand places within India, eventually became famous as "bleeding India with a thousand cuts".

Pakistan knew they could never beat India in a direct fight, hence attack through paid mercenaries, across hundreds of different locations within India, so that it becomes physically impossible for India to give a coordinated response. It does sound similar to the KMG plan. In the first sentence at the beginning of this paragraph, one just has to replace the following words – Pakistan with opposition, India with Modi, paid mercenaries with joint opposition candidate, and locations with parliamentary constituencies. And voila!

Opposition knew they could never beat Modi in a direct fight, hence attack through joint opposition candidates across different parliamentary constituencies, so that it becomes physically impossible for Modi to give a coordinated response.

Perhaps the KMG drew inspiration from Zia-ul-Haq's theory of bleeding India with a thousand cuts. In all likelihood, they had taken a leaf out of his book and had come up with their own indigenous version "Bleed Modi with 543 cuts" plan.

While Modi had banished the KMG and Lutyen's media from its proximity to power, they continued to thrive, as their roots run deep, given that they have spread their tentacles across the ecosystem. He would surely know that and perhaps, was ready for a longer haul. Modi had blown the bugle by jettisoning the KMG and sidelining Lutyen's media. Perhaps for the first time in democratic India, a man had challenged the dynastic order. War had been declared, and it was not just a battle to end the perpetuation of a dynasty or to win 2019, but a war for the narrative of the 'Idea of India'!

# 2
# The Genesis of Mahagathbandhan

This has been the first time in the political history of independent India that the whole opposition, for its own survival, was keen to unite against one person. Bitter foes were to become inseparable friends, sworn enemies would eat from each other's hands, people who were at each other's throats were soon going to fall into a never-to-be-broken tight embrace, or atleast till the 2019 general elections got over!

Why did the Modi-led NDA 2 government face such a fierce opposition? It is not that we had the BJP/NDA government for the first time. We had the Vajpayee-led NDA 1, which had a smooth run and there was never such a concerted effort by the combined opposition to dislodge him. It obviously had to do with the leadership. While both Vajpayee and Modi were bred in the same ideology, both were RSS *pracharaks* (volunteers), both great orators, yet they were very distinct personalities, which seem to have led to such a contrasting response by the opposition. Hence, before we get to the reasons for such a divergent response, it will be interesting to get a quick snapshot into their varied personalities. Enough about both these individuals is in the public domain for a keen student of behavioural science to assess their personalities fairly accurately.

Decision-making is a key requirement of any leader. In fact, the higher one climbs up the hierarchy, the more important the decision-making skill becomes. Hence, for a top role in a country, decision-making becomes the most crucial aspect, a make all or break all. Broadly, one keeps two aspects in mind while taking decisions – First, of course is, what is the right thing to do? Second is, how does it affect others?

All key decisions one makes, in addition to considering what the right thing to do is, one also thinks what will others think and/or feel about this decision of mine. Some of us do more of the former and some consider more of the latter as we make our decisions. The degree will vary from person to person. Some would even be on the extremes – either always doing the right thing without bothering what others would feel, or being so bothered about what others will think or feel that either they will not take the decision or delay it, or take a call that keeps everyone happy. Now let us weigh Modi and Vajpayee on this parameter.

Modi seems to take decisions in an impersonal way. His actions appear to be based on logical reasoning and he appears to be keen to do the right thing. Vajpayee appeared to give higher weightage in his decision-making to how others felt about it and how they were affected with it. Modi appears to value the right thing and fairness a lot more, while Vajpayee seemed to value harmonious relations, accommodating a lot more. Modi is generally described as logical, rational, means business, hard taskmaster and decisive, while Vajpayee was more known for his warmth, empathy, leisureliness and expedience. Leaders like

Modi can be categorised more as the rational type while Vajpayee more as the emotional type. It does not mean that a person will have one at the exclusion of the other; it just means that one of the quotients, rational or emotional, is more dominant than the other.

Let us quickly read through a couple of examples to elaborate on this.

If one considers Demonetisation and Balakot strikes, they highlight Modi's determined and single-minded focus on doing the right thing, no matter what it takes. These were highly impersonal decisions, which had a very high probability of failure, which could have led to his political demise. Demonetisation was going to cause inconvenience to millions of people and Balakot strikes had the potential of escalating the hostility with Pakistan. Many folks called them reckless decisions, yet he succeeded both times and how! That is because he had logically thought through the pros and cons as well as the consequences. They were calculative risks but deeply analysed by an extremely sharp mind.

A lot has been talked about two incidents during Vajpayee's time – Kandahar hijack and Lahore bus ride. Both highlight how much he cared about feelings, emotions and connections. On Kandahar, Vajpayee would have definitely known the long-term consequences of releasing the terrorists, but he just could not ignore the human angle staring at his face in that trying phase. The fact that the opposition jointly also recommended the release would have further appealed to his empathetic faculties. These decisions surprised many, given BJP's overall rather hawkish approach on terrorism. Decisions such as these may have been the reasons behind his critics as well as some BJP hardliners labelling Vajpayee of a *mukhauta* (mask).

Hence, for Modi, fairness and the right thing appears to trump everything else. He seems to have a strong sense of justice and if he is convinced of the correctness of a particular path, he will follow it, even if he knows it may harm him. More often than not, he will take the right path rather than an expedient one.

Now coming to the reasons for the Mahagathbandhan. Ostensibly, the reason given was that the constitutional institutions were being destroyed and that democracy was in danger due to Modi's dictatorial approach. Both these stated reasons never really cut much ice with the public at large. Because, one, the opposition could never provide any shred of evidence; and second, the dismal track record of the opposition in both these areas. People still had not forgotten the Emergency days and closer still, the memories of Rahul tearing away the ordinance, in full public gaze, passed by the then Prime Minister and the cabinet of his own party was still fresh in the minds of the public.

So what could have been the real reasons for the creation of Mahagathbandhan? In the context of the decision-making styles of both Modi and Vajpayee above, it will become easier to appreciate and understand the points being made below.

First, Modi had started challenging the Nehruvian order. While maintaining Gandhi's pre-eminent position as the undisputed leader of modern India, he accorded the next pedestal to leaders like Subhash Chandra Bose, Sardar Patel, Dr B.R. Ambedkar, among others, in addition to Nehru. This was in sharp contrast to the approach followed by the earlier governments, including Vajpayee, where Nehru was the unchallenged second after Bapu. Vajpayee skirted this issue and never disturbed the order. Modi, on the other hand, was determined to give the deserving leaders their rightful place.

In order to further perpetuate and fortify Nehru's legacy, the KMG propagated an idea of India that laid more stress on the post-Independence India where obviously Nehru, by the virtue of having been the first prime minister, had a huge impact. Over time, this brought rich political dividends to the dynasty. Modi started bringing a new narrative by invoking India's rich cultural heritage with his frequent references to ancient India's rich culture as well as its past heroes. Getting Yoga acknowledged on the global platform as a rich Indian tradition which can benefit humanity at large is one such example.

As discussed earlier, one of the vestiges of the Nehruvian order, the KMG and the Lutyen's media were completely sidelined and rooted out from the top echelons of power in one fell swoop. Even though they would have been at odds with Vajpayee too, however, he being as accommodative as he was; he kept them in good humour and never tried to unsettle them.

Second, there was perhaps an unwritten rule amongst the political parties to overlook corrupt practises of leaders, especially at the top of the pecking order of a party. That is apparently why, ever since Independence, while there have been numerous corruption scandals at the highest levels, hardly anyone noteworthy was ever convicted. At best, you would see a few babus, those too very far and few, who were held responsible. Modi changed all that and decided to spare none. Top political leaders, across parties, started getting booked; it seemed to spook the political class.

Modi would have known that he would be stirring up the hornet's nest by striking at the most formidable elitist political legacy, by challenging the Nehruvian order, as well as the all-powerful elitist political class by pursuing corruption investigations against political leaders, he was demolishing the political order too. However, as is his wont, he was determined to do the 'right' thing, unconcerned with the negative consequences that may fall upon him. The bonhomie at the top echelons of the political class had been shattered. It is nice to have bonhomie with all, but when it goes to the extent of overlooking each other's sins, it is unethical and hence undesirable. The bonhomie existed perhaps just for the purpose of scratching each other's back.

Lastly, realpolitik would have been a key reason. Despite all the bravado showcased by all political parties of how certain they were of defeating Modi in 2019, in their heart of hearts, they knew that Modi had surpassed not only Vajpayee, but had become so popular and strong that it was next to impossible for any one or two of them to beat him. Hence, the decision seemed to be more out of necessity rather than any conviction whatsoever.

For the Congress and Left parties, the first reason seemed to be the driving force to bring everyone together. How could anyone challenge the dynasty and its idol, Nehru? For the parties whose leaders were facing corruption charges, the second reason obviously trumped everything else. All parties knew that Modi's popularity was phenomenal among the people and the opposition parties had no scope of winning unless they came together. Hence, Modi had actually himself become a strong glue for a 'Mahagathbandhan'. Modi had the penchant of taking the bull by the horns, and he had the enormous support of the masses behind him, the kind that Vajpayee never had.

# 3
# Modi's Bali Effect

From 2004 up to 2014 during the UPA regime, the central investigative agencies put Modi through intense scrutiny, consisting of enquiries against him at various levels for the Gujarat riots, including a physical questioning session lasting for over eight hours. All this while he was holding the office of the Chief Minister. He withstood this with stoic dignity, without any sense of retribution. Lutyen's media led a relentless campaign against Modi, did a trial of its own and pronounced him guilty even before the case reached the courts. One must remember that in those days, the media industry had not opened up and Lutyen's media lorded all over it. Hence, it did not take them long to demonise Modi. The web of inquiries, investigations and scrutiny ensured that media would play up the matter and keep it fresh in public memory. Despite this, he continued to win Gujarat, election after election, and had an unbroken winning streak from 2002 to 2014, subsequent to which he became the Prime Minister of the country. He was eventually exonerated by the highest court of the land for Gujarat riots.

Another major flash point between him and the central government was the Ishrat Jahan encounter case. The encounter took place in 2004 and was alleged that it was a fake one. The High Court of Gujarat ordered an inquiry. In August 2009, the union home ministry first filed an affidavit with the court in which it claimed that Ishrat Jahan was "actively associated with Lashkar-e-Taiba, a Pakistan-based terrorist organisation. However, mysteriously in September 2009, the union home ministry withdrew the first affidavit and filed a second affidavit with the court, reversing their earlier position on the ground that its earlier claim was not based on conclusive intelligence inputs. It further mentioned that the evidence previously used to link her to LeT was needlessly misinterpreted.

BJP immediately cried foul and alleged that the central government was trying to discredit the state government by raising false allegations on the encounter and soiling Modi's reputation. Incidentally, Amit Shah, the then Home Minister of Gujarat, went to jail for this case. Ultimately, Shah was acquitted. Not withstanding all this, Modi grew from strength to strength and continued his victory march unabated. It had slowly but surely started dawning on the political pundits that all these invectives and allegations being hurled by Modi's opposition was proving counter-productive and actually helping him to gain public sympathy and support.

Talking about invectives, there is this story about the islanders of Solomon Islands in the pacific who are supposed to follow a unique practise. Whenever they need to cut a tree, which is too big to chop down, they surround the tree and curse it for hours on end every day. After a few weeks, or months, the tree dies and falls on the ground. It is believed that the negative energy emanating from the curses damages the life energy of the tree, which brings the downfall. Aamir Khan referred to this story in his much-acclaimed movie *Taare Zameen Par* in 2007. While no one has been able to prove the veracity of this claim, it seems that the Congress party and the KMG took this story very seriously.

Right from the Gujarat elections in 2007, starting with Maut ka Saudagar (merchant of death) to Bhasmasur (a demon that could turn you to ashes with just a touch), the Congress party had been hurling choicest of abuses at Modi till the run up to the 2014 elections, and even beyond. Perhaps not a single demon from our ancient scriptures or the lowliest of the creatures from animal kingdom was spared from being equated with Modi with a desperate hope that eventually Modi will fall.

On the other hand, just as the 'Maut ka Saudagar' comment by Sonia Gandhi was widely thought to have laid the foundation of Modi's victory in Gujarat state election in 2007, Mani Shankar Aiyar's 'Chaiwala' jibe was thought to have given a major fillip to Modi's campaign in 2014. Aiyar had famously commented, "In this 21st century, I promise you, Modi will never ever become the Prime Minister. Instead, if he wants to distribute tea, we will make some space for him at this Congress conclave." Aiyar said this while attending a Congress conclave in January 2014. Within no time, Modi upped the ante and his humble chaiwala background became the backdrop of his immensely popular campaign of which 'Chai pe Chercha' was one of the key events.

It seemed Aiyar did not learn his lessons from 2014 and launched another tirade at Modi on the eve of Gujarat elections in December 2017. He called him a *neech aadmi* (a lowly person). This was a time when Congress was giving a tough fight to BJP and some opinion surveys were even suggesting that

Congress was in a winning position in Gujarat. Eventually, BJP won the election.

It was not just invectives that were being hurled at Modi; his opponents would show their immense hatred for him by menacingly uttering how they would go about physically brutalising him. One Congress leader, Imran Masood from UP was caught on tape in March 2014, publicly saying that he will chop Modi into pieces while addressing a rally. In November 2017, Tej Pratap, Lalu Prasad Yadav's son, thundered, "Modi *ki khaal udhadvalenge hum*." (We will get Modi scalped). Such gruesome threats seemed to be becoming par a way of life for the opposition.

Perhaps no politician other than Modi has ever been subjected to such a concerted and vicious campaign to besmirch his image. In Modi's case, it had been going on ever since 2002. One must give credit to KMG for their foresight. They could see, very early on, what others could not. They could see a crusader in him. They could see then that this man, Modi, had the potential and capability to challenge the Nehruvian order!

Now imagine this picture – a politician who is 24/7, vilified by the opposing political class, demonised by media, hated and accused by influential lobbies and KMG, and hounded by the law enforcement agencies with all kinds of cases, not just survives but thrives through all this. Any politician, the most brilliant one at that, would have been finished long ago, but not Modi. Public image is the most critical factor that makes or breaks any politician and a concerted onslaught by either the political class, or press, or the influential intelligentsia or the authorities would have dealt a fatal blow. In Modi's case, it seemed to be a combined effort by all these forces, and yet, he maintained a continuous political victory run ever since 2001, eventually going on to hold the top most position of our republic! There has to be something wrong with this picture. How is this just possible? The man has to have some supernatural powers by his side, so would one imagine…

Bali was a powerful monkey king, elder brother of Sugriva who subsequently helped Lord Ram defeat Ravan. Now for some reason, Sugriva was thrown out of the kingdom by Bali. To make matters worse, he forcefully took Sugriva's wife as his own. Hence, Sugriva reached out to Ram to deliver justice and help him win back his wife and kingdom. To cut the long story short, eventually Ram killed Bali, but he had to do it with stealth, without coming face to face with him. Why? Because Bali had a boon from Brahma, that in any duel with Bali, as soon as his opponent comes face to face for a fight, he would lose half his strength to Bali, which meant that even god, in the form of Ram, could not defeat him face to face in an open dual. Maybe, Modi possesses such a boon, maybe the opponents need to be beware of this Bali effect.

# 4
# The Illusionists

As per the dictionary, an illusionist is someone who performs tricks that deceive the eye. Another description states an illusionist performs tricks where objects seem to appear and then disappear.

It all started with an author, Uday Prakash, who, on 4 September 2015 returned his Sahitya Akademi award as a mark of protest against the murder of M.M. Kulbargi, a rationalist scholar and an award winner. He was murdered in August in Bengaluru. Subsequently, a mob-lynching incident was reported from Dadri, Uttar Pradesh (UP), where a Muslim man was killed allegedly for eating and storing beef at his residence. It led to a spate of award-returning incidents – that was popularly known as award *wapsi* – where around forty odd award-winning artists and intellectuals returned their awards to the central government.

It did not dawn on these celebrities that the Kulbargi assassination happened in Karnataka, then ruled by Congress-JDS alliance and the Dadri incident was under the Samajwadi Party government in UP. Law and order is a state subject but all the ire was being directed at Modi.

These were authors, poets, film-makers, playwrights, among others, all protesting against the growing intolerance and government's silence on it. Some of the comments being made were as follows:

"The country is passing through very tough times. It's worse than Emergency".

"We are going backwards. There is rising intolerance."

The sudden rush of returning awards took people by surprise. It was suggested that a lot of them were returning these awards to get into the limelight. Lutyen's media's role was most crucial and critical in this controversy. These topics were making headlines all the time during that phase. Each artist, who returned his or her award, would get a pride of place in the publications or news channels. Editorials and prime time debates on electronic media were busy equating Modi government to fascist regimes of yore. It seemed as if there was nothing else happening in the country but lynching and communal violence, presided by an oppressive government.

Then one fine day, suddenly this controversy disappeared. Everything was back to normal as it was before the issue erupted. In fact, Uday Prakash, the author who started it all, in early December 2015, went on to profusely praise Modi for his speech in Parliament on the subject. Analysts scrambled to understand what exactly had just happened. Then someone suddenly realised that Bihar elections had just concluded and the Mahagathbandhan had won. It seemed the goal had been achieved!

Later on, during saner times the next year, *Economic Times* in its 25 February 2016 edition, compared figures of communal incidents of last twenty months of NDA government until

January 2016 with the corresponding period of the last twenty months of the UPA regime. Incidentally, exactly the same number of incidents, 1222, were reported in both periods. Therefore, in addition to the fact that maintaining public order is a state subject, country-wide too there was no spike. As most had suspected, it was more to do with the social ills that had plagued the country since long, and had nothing to do with the Modi government.

A certain section of intellectuals were later accused of having colluded with the media to create this baseless controversy. In hindsight, the accusation did not seem baseless, as a similar pattern would play out in other instances later. A few people would start a protest or an agitation. Lutyen's media would give it front page headlines and project it as if it is a nation-wide angst. The electronic media would take the que and run prime-time debates on the subject and a perception would be created that the whole nation is gripped with it. After some time, just when it would seem that the issue had died down, perhaps to give it legs, suddenly we'd see a few ex-bureaucrats, invariably from the erstwhile UPA era, coming together and writing an open letter to the Prime Minister, expressing concern over the same subject matter. It promptly makes front-page headlines, courtesy Lutyen's media, seemingly just to prove the sustainability of an issue that was already flogged to death. The illusion of intolerance has thus been conjured.

It seemed to be a fairly well-orchestrated ploy by the KMG to discredit the government. KMG in partnership with Lutyen's media seemed to have perfected the art of conjuring up illusions, not just for the perpetuation of the dynasty, but also to bring down anyone who became a threat to it. This was the greatest weapon in their hands, and a dangerous one at that. In the world of politics, image can make or mar a leader. KMG knew they had a big lever and they were going to leverage it to continue testing Modi's Bali effect.

Media is a conscience keeper of a society and critical for the smooth functioning of a democracy. That is why it is also called as the fourth pillar of democracy. However, it also has the tendency to degenerate into a manipulator who selectively presents news to create an illusion and misguide the minds of people for ulterior motives. Media's quest should be the search for truth, not to conjure up alternative truths. Its role is that of an illuminator, not an illusionist.

# 5
# Congress – The unmissable turn Left

## *Suit boot ki Sarkar*

One accusation that perhaps did have an effect on Modi – to the extent that it seemingly altered the course of his economic agenda and hence was a significant event during his first term – was the "Suit boot ki Sarkar" (Government of the rich and mighty) jibe by Rahul Gandhi. This swipe was about Modi's monogrammed pinstriped suit he wore during Obama's India visit.

One of Modi's key economic agendas was to promote setting up of manufacturing units and provide a major impetus to the Make in India programme. However, one of the major barriers was land acquisition.The Land Acquisition, Rehabilitation and Resettlement Act 2013, made it extremely tedious and cumbersome for industries to acquire land and had become a big hurdle in promoting industry and infrastructure development. Hence, towards the end of 2014, the Modi government promulgated an ordinance, which did away with certain stringent clauses for industrial corridors, Public-Private Partnership projects, rural infrastructure, affordable housing, and defence projects. The amendment bill was introduced in Parliament and while it was passed in Lok Sabha, NDA came under heavy attack from the opposition, both inside and outside the parliament, for being 'pro-corporate houses' and 'anti-farmer'.

Rahul Gandhi was quick to seize the opportunity and led a spirited "Suit boot ki Sarkar" attack. He alleged that Modi's bonhomie with big corporate houses was at the cost of overlooking the agrarian distress spread across the country. This was a hard-hitting and relentless campaign, which had the potential to damage Modi government's image. It seems Modi, an astute politician that he was, perhaps sensed the headwinds blowing his way and realised the need for an appropriate response. The sequence of events certainly point in that direction.

Modi allowed the land amendment bill to lapse and did not pursue it any further. An aggressive Public Sector Undertaking disinvestment plan was also put on the back-burner. Modi turned his complete attention and focus on to the many welfare schemes launched by the government. He brought in an even higher level of urgency and rigour in its implementation. The housing scheme for the rural poor was relaunched to improve speed, quality and delivery while new schemes like affordable housing for urban poor and Ujjwala Yojana were launched. A mega loan scheme for the weaker sections of the society called Mudra Yojana was launched with a view to "fund the unfunded" and help the poor to start their own micro/small businesses.

This perhaps was a rare step back and a midway course correction by Modi. It seemed he had planned a double booster doze for welfare schemes as well as the industry. However, Modi has this unique ability to sense the political environment like no other politician does, and decided to halt the booster for manufacturing, apparently for a more opportune time, and instead shift his focus completely towards welfare schemes. This move would go on to prove critical for his campaign in 2019. This was another example of his uncanny knack of converting a challenge into an opportunity.

## *Tukre Tukre gang*

Students of Jawaharlal Nehru University always punch much above their weight. The institution has close to eight thousand students, but the kind of press they get during their student elections, any outsider would confuse it as a key barometer of nation's electoral mood. On the other hand, its poor cousin, Delhi University student elections, which houses over two lakh students, are passed off by the press as just another student elections! Hence, it was not really a surprise to see an event at JNU shaking the whole nation as media channels swarmed it for a few days in February 2016.

A protest was organised by a left wing student union against the death penalty of Afzal Guru, accused and convicted for the attack on Parliament in 2001. While permission was denied by the authorities, students went ahead with the protest. The event resulted in clashes between the left and right wing students. Thanks to technology, the event highlights were captured by some students on their respective phones, which were promptly passed on to media houses who gleefully relayed the same to the whole nation. What seemed obvious from the videos was that the platform was also used to raise anti-India slogans, the most iconic ones being – "*Bharat tere tukre honge*", and "*Azadi*".

When translated they read as "India will be broken into pieces" and "freedom", respectively. The leaders who organised the protest were arrested on charges of sedition and were later released on bail.

The opposition parties led by the Congress sensed an opportunity to browbeat Modi, as this incident seemed to fit in with the illusion of 'intolerance' earlier conjured up by KMG. They provided unequivocal support to the 'Tukre Tukre Gang', a term which would henceforth be popularly used for the students who shouted those slogans at JNU as well as all the left liberals and intellectuals who supported them. Their leaders actually descended on to the JNU campus to be physically present alongside the agitating students. Rahul Gandhi was one of the first to visit the campus and there was a beeline of Aam Aadmi, left and other party leaders visiting the campus to register their support as well as to oppose the government's action.

The whole episode, since it played out in front of the whole nation, had one positive unintended outcome. It triggered a debate on the issue of nationalism and brought internal security to the fore, which had not taken centre stage until then in Modi's term. Slowly but surely, in full public gaze, two sharply contrasting views started emerging, making it easier for the citizens to distinguish between the two and make an informed choice. The issue of nationalism, which henceforth had become a part of popular perception of the aspirational India, was to go right up to the elections and beyond.

The student arrests were termed by the opposition as further proof of the government's intolerance while the government pointed to the template of the event being used as inspiration by the separatists and stonepelters in Kashmir. As these discussions gathered steam, another issue related to urban naxals started getting played out, highlighting the various breakaway tendencies that were plaguing the nation.

Over more than a decade, our internal security agencies were making steady progress curbing the scourge of naxalism in the country. However, it is the Modi government which took the fight to the next level and started cracking down on the ideological as well as financial support ecosystem of the Naxalite movement, right in the heart of India's most urban areas. Many institutions under the garb of NGOs that were allegedly supporting the nefarious activities were either shut down or put on notice. For the first time, intellectuals working as human rights lawyers, academics, etc., were booked for conspiring to create unrest across the country and taken to task. It was well known that in earlier times such groups operated under the overall protection of the state, swear as they did ostensibly, to the Nehruvian ideals. Now, they were being exposed.

On this issue too, the Congress party took a diametrically opposite view to the no-nonsense stance of the government and chose to support the cause of all the agencies/NGOs and people who were booked by the government for supporting naxalism and vehemently criticised the government for the harsh action. The debate got shriller as the differentiated stands of the two opponents – BJP/NDA and the rest – became clear. Battle lines were drawn. Thanks to the tukre tukre gang, the issue of national security had come centre stage, right into the drawing room of ordinary citizens and to the advantage of BJP. It further fortified Modi's image as that of a strong and decisive leader. Henceforth, BJP would showcase the nationalist tag proudly on their chests. In hindsight, this would turn out to be the net practise for the final game on national security narrative, which eventually played out during the general elections of 2019.

The term 'nationalist' became so popular that a few of the most watched news channels started identifying themselves with that tag and underlined it as their sworn ethos, to good effect.

Another outcome of these two unrelated events – suit boot ki Sarkar and Bharat tere tukre honge – was the near complete irrelevance of the Left front as Rahul Gandhi appropriated their agenda. In the first instance, it was Rahul Gandhi who led a spirited anti-capitalist campaign, resulting in successfully thwarting the land acquisition amendment bill. He relentlessly tried to create an impression that Modi was working in close proximity with a few top business tycoons. He often took jibes and criticised him, trying to cultivate a pro-farmer, pro-poor image of himself.

In the second instance, while the whole drama was initiated by the left wing students of JNU, the lasting image that would get etched in the minds of the public was of Rahul Gandhi standing next to them at the campus in support of their agitation. Congress not just physically and morally supported the students, but eventually went on to adopt an extreme left stance in their manifesto for 2019, by promising to scrap the sedition law, as well as curtail the powers of the Army in the case of AFSPA (Armed Forces Special Powers Act) being enforced in disturbed areas like Kashmir. Left again seemed to be just a helpless bystander. These two events marked Congress's unmissable turn towards Left.

Congress's bandwagon had taken a decisive turn to the left and taken the road already traversed by them. Both would henceforth fight for more or less the same voter base, which was shrinking quickly. Hence, the situation was that both were chugging along side by side on a road, which was narrowing as they moved ahead. Eventually, at some point of time, the road would have become so narrow, leading to a collision between the two and as a result, a probable scenario of both being thrown off the track. Only time will tell the extent of damage to both the bandwagons, but one thing was sure – if they continued on this track, they were heading for an unmitigated disaster.

# 6
# 56-inch chest, finally bared

## *Surgical Strikes*

Midway through Modi's term, the overall macro-economic indicators were looking good, GDP was growing at a healthy clip, inflation was well in control and foreign direct investments were growing even though the big ticket economic reforms like disinvestment and land reforms were put on the back burner. Modi's flagship programmes like Swachh Bharat and Jan Dhan Yojana were gaining traction on the ground, taking tremendous strides. Politically, BJP had won states of Jharkhand, Haryana, Maharashtra, Assam, formed a coalition government with PDP in Jammu & Kashmir and added on to their kitty of governing states. Delhi and Bihar were a setback where they had hoped to wrest power but were unable to do so. Overall, BJP had made significant headway in expanding its footprint across India and had splashed more of orange across the landscape, especially the Northeast.

However, there were a couple of issues that were catching a lot of media glare, had provided a stick to the opposition to attack the government with and take jibes at Modi, calling out for his 56-inch chest at every given opportunity. During election campaign in 2014, Modi had highlighted the poor track record of Samajwadi Party's development record in UP, took a dig at Mulayam Singh, and said that one needs a '56-inch chest' to develop a state, like he had done in Gujarat. From the moment Modi won in 2014, the opposition, at every alleged failing of Modi, would invoke his 56-inch chest.

The one issue that Modi heard this jibe most on was Pakistan. Modi had started on a positive and conciliatory note with Pakistan. Modi offered a hand of friendship to Nawaz Sharif initially by inviting him to his swearing-in ceremony and later on by making an unscheduled visit in late December 2015 to Lahore to meet Nawaz on the occasion of his grand daughter's wedding. However, this bonhomie was short-lived.

Within a week of Modi's visit to Pakistan, a terrorist attack was launched at Pathankot Air Force station by Jaish-e-Mohammad, a Pakistan-based terrorist group. In this attack, one civilian died and seven of our security personnel were martyred. Unfortunately, such a deceitful attitude by Pakistan was not on display for the first time. During NDA1, Vajpayee's extension of an olive branch by taking a bus ride to Lahore was met with hostility at Kargil by the then Pakistan government. Modi was accused by the opposition for not learning his lessons from the past and falling into a trap of his own making.

The opposition would go on to allege that Modi's approach at this instance was at odds with the stated tough stance of BJP vis-a-vis Pakistan. Modi was criticised for his alleged confused policy with respect to Pakistan and the opposition constantly taunted him by invoking his 56-inch chest, daring him to give a strong response. Such political potshots would go on for another few months until the Uri attack happened in mid-September

2016. This attack was reported as the deadliest one on security forces in the past couple of decades, in which 19 soldiers lost their lives. After this, the opposition criticism became more strident. The nation too was exasperated and getting impatient with the government. Modi would have realised that it cannot be business as usual from then on, and something concrete had to be done. So he publicly stated his intent to seek retribution this time.

India's Pakistan policy up to that time had been of utmost restraint, and even in instances of extreme provocation like the Mumbai attacks, India never crossed the line. Other than vehemently denouncing the barbaric acts and sending proofs to Pakistan of its own territory being used for launching such attacks on India, precious little had been done. Even during Kargil, though Pakistan was the aggressor who had infiltrated our borders, India never crossed the LOC as we successfully pushed them back. So irrespective of who was in power, NDA or the UPA, the policy followed consistently was that of maximum restraint. In such a scenario, people were wondering if at all India will break the tradition of restraint. If it did, what would it actually do? India did not have to wait for long to get the answer.

On 29 September 2016, India woke up stunned by a new lexicon called "Surgical Strikes". In the wee hours that day, Indian forces had gone deep inside Pakistan occupied Kashmir (PoK) and demolished terror launch pads. It was estimated that anywhere close to 35 to 70 terrorists were killed. To top it, all Indian soldiers had safely returned to their bases in India after successfully completing the operation. This marked a significant departure from the past and gave a big fillip to Modi's strong-man image.

On its part, Opposition – especially the Congress – made a grave error in the way they responded to this tectonic shift in India's policy. If one looks at it objectively, this whole operation had to be looked at in two distinct parts. One part was the decision made to conduct surgical strikes, which was a political call taken by Modi. The second part was the execution that the Army had carried out. Now for the opposition to respond politically, they should have restricted themselves to the first part, which was the decision by Modi. Instead, they treaded into the out-of-bounds territory by doubting the success of the strikes. Even worse, actually questioning if at all the strikes happened.

By doing this, they ended up undermining the Army and actually toeing the Pakistan line, which BJP exploited to the fullest. It was quite evident that the opposition had messed up and lost the perception battle in the minds of the public.

There were three possible appropriate response options for the opposition. One, they could have criticised Modi for going against the established doctrine of maximum restraint which was a considered policy thus far, given that Pakistan is a nuclear state and an unpredictable one. They could have pitched it as – this could easily escalate into a full-blown war, which both the countries could ill afford. However, this approach would have gone against the mood prevalent in the nation during that time. People were getting impatient and wanted an appropriate aggressive response.

Second, the opposition could have welcomed and celebrated the strikes along with the government and the nation. However, this would have meant going against their 'anti-Modi at any cost' policy. But more importantly, electorally perhaps they were concerned about a section of their vote bank who they imagined will go against them, if they were to support a belligerent line against Pakistan.

The third approach could have been that they took an even more hawkish approach. While welcoming this move, they could have said that the response needed to be stronger. However, this would have gone completely against the grain of Congress, which always had Left leanings. Moreover, in recent times, they had turned completely left on most of the issues. Hence, it would have been incongruent for them to take this stand.

Of the three approaches, it would be evident to any student of politics that the first response would have been more in line with the opposition's philosophy. After all, policy of maximum restraint and peaceful existence was the one of the higher ideals of Nehru that Congress as well as most in the opposition always swore by. However, it seems they just did not have the courage of conviction to state this, clearly fearing a backlash from a big section of voters, and perhaps a sizable one at that. Instead, they kept beating around the bush and ended up tying themselves up in knots.

It will be instructive to note here that one of the critical lessons taught in leadership is that you can never make everyone happy all the time. When a party finds it expedient not to take a stand fearing losing support of a section of people, it ends up eroding its support among some other section of people. The next time around, on some other issue, it again vacillates and ends up eroding its base in another section. This leads to shrinking of its base over time. Unknowingly, Congress was digging its own grave. They were in dire need to learn this lesson.

Surgical strikes were a radical shift in India's Pakistan policy. India had sent a clear message that henceforth, we reserve the right to launch pre-emptive strikes across the Line of Control (LoC) to defend against imminent attacks. The fact that the communication was worded in a way that clearly conveyed that the action was in self-defence, it ensured that these strikes were well within the parameters of international law. It was a clear departure from the erstwhile UPA policy of maximum restraint with Pakistan. Modi had raised the stakes for Pakistan in case of any future misadventures by jihadi elements from Pakistan. He had forced them to rethink their policy of 'bleed India by a thousand cuts'!

## *Demonetisation*

The second issue that would have perhaps had Modi in a bit of bother was that of corruption. The first decision Modi government made was to set up a Special Investigating Team (SIT) to unearth black money. The earlier UPA government had deferred despite the Supreme Court's order to set it up way back in 2011. In addition, the government carried out various steps to root out corruption and tackle the menace of black money by making new laws or amending current ones like benami property act, the bankruptcy code, income declaration schemes, double taxation avoidance agreement, among other. However, all this was overshadowed when Vijay Mallya fled from the country in March 2016. Opposition did not lose any opportunity to milk this and lay the blame at Modi's doorstep.

This was bad optics for Modi, who came to power primarily on the governance agenda. Even though there was not a single charge of corruption against the Modi regime, there was an expectation that something more concrete would be done. It was clear that getting back black money from abroad was a complex process, which would take a lot of time and effort. However, the other point was that the black economy within the country was thriving and somehow brakes had to be applied on it. With this backdrop, on 8 November 2016, at 8:00 p.m. in a televised address to the nation, Modi declared illegal all currency notes of 500 and 1000 denomination. Indians, just before they slept that night, were sensitised to a relatively unheard of word thus far, "Demonetisation".

India is an emotionally demonstrative country. We wear emotions on our sleeves. We agitate, protest, block roads, trains and bring life to a grinding halt at the smallest of pretexts. Yet, such a disruptive step which was causing inconvenience and hardship to crores and crores of Indians, not just for a few days but months, did not even attract a single protest by a common man. It was nothing short of phenomenal. Even more amazing is the fact that this aspect never got the media attention that it deserved. However, it would be instructive to understand a few seemingly obvious reasons behind the peace and calm.

Firstly, irrespective of studies conducted by various credible sources putting a figure on black economy in India to anywhere between 40% to even upwards of 70%, common man did not need experts to tell him that. He saw brazen display of black money with his own eyes all around him. At weddings, in hotels, on roads, in shops, in houses, in fancy real estates – there were ostensible demonstrations everywhere. It was a well-known fact that for any property deal, people had to dish out around 50% or more in cash. Hence, it was not just that the black money was thriving, but actually even honest people were left with no option but to indulge in such unethical practices. The poor saw it, the middle class saw it and even the law-abiding rich saw it, detested it and wanted the government to do something about it.

Secondly, people generally understood that the malice was so deep that it needed an extraordinary step. They understood that the matter was so complex that no government had ever been able to do anything about it and it needed a tough call. Standing in queues, it was not surprising to hear many people say that it was high time such a step was taken and they were prepared to face the hardships.

Thirdly, people had hope. People felt that something good would come out of this exercise. In fact, many people felt that standing in queues and facing inconvenience was their way of contributing towards this noble cause of weeding out black money.

Fourthly, there is enough anecdotal evidence to conclude that black money hoarders were indeed hassled and people could see that. There were reports of how notes were either being burnt or were being thrown away in rivers. Almost everyone had a story to tell about how inconvenienced hoarders were and at what lengths they were going to either get rid or save their ill-gotten wealth. For a change, a hoarder was at the receiving end and an honest person was sitting pretty. The tables seemed to have turned.

Fifthly, poor seemed to have actually benefitted from this situation. There were enough media reports of how hoarders were approaching poor to deposit cash in their accounts, which they would return later, of course after a hefty cut. There were reports of people standing in queues on behalf of rich for a fee. It was widely reported that many businesses in the informal sector paid off their workers a few months of wages in advance and asked them to return to their villages as they shut shop temporarily. Not for no reason, Modi during one of the election rallies immediately after demonetisation exhorted the audience, constituting majority of poor people, not to return the money that had been deposited in their accounts by the hoarders. Of course, we will never know formally or officially what was the exact scale, but if we were to look at just one concrete indicator, we perhaps can reasonably conclude that actually redistribution of wealth was happening all the time during this phase itself. Two-wheeler sales in India are mostly on cash and hence an accurate barometer of purchasing power of people in the lower economic strata. In 2017-18, which followed the year in which demonetisation happened, two-wheeler sales grew by a huge 14.8%. Growth in the preceding couple of years was 6-7% only.

Lastly and most importantly, credibility of Modi was a key factor. Modi's image as a clear administrator had further enhanced in the two-and-a-half years as the Prime Minister. People saw him as a sincere, hard-working, selfless person who worked round the clock for the betterment of India and its people. Citizens recognised that it was a tough call for Modi, which put his own political existence at risk, and people appreciated that. People trusted Modi on this.

It was a combination of all the factors elaborated above that perhaps the most disruptive exercise ever conducted by the government in India's history, certainly from a common citizen's convenience standpoint, went through in a most systematic, disciplined and smooth manner, without any obstacles. Ironically, the only segment that protested was the political class in the opposition.

Demonetisation was actually the first time when all the opposition leaders came together in one frame to protest against this alleged draconian move. Imagine what impression a common person would draw from this picture. He saw the hoarders harassed by demonetisation and now he was seeing all the opposition leaders anguished and protesting. No wonder Modi fully exploited this frame as he went around, rally after rally, claiming that the only people unhappy with demonetisation were the hoarders and the opposition leaders. The point had hit home!

Demonetisation would have been a fascinating exercise, especially for the students of organisation transformation and human behaviour. Transformations are never easy and most of them fail, especially the disruptive ones. Primarily because there is a science behind it, which most people do not follow. Here we had a countrywide disruptive transformation that was successfully executed. It succeeded because people clearly saw and felt the need and were completely aligned with it. They saw an end state, which was positive, it was communicated well and a trusted leader led it from the front.

Modi also came under a lot of fire for announcing the scheme himself rather than letting the finance minister or even the finance secretary do it. Any student of leadership and management would tell you that it would have been a grave mistake. A transformation planned at such a massive scale, which was going to affect the whole country and its entire population, had to be launched by none other than the top leader, the Prime Minister. We perhaps would never know if Modi took advice from a management expert before he went for this initiative, but he certainly did tick all the boxes on all the key elements that the specialist would have advised him.

Surgical strikes and demonetisation also gave a major boost to the BJP cadre and gave them talking points with which they could effectively respond to the opposition. The tables had started turning and BJP supporters were back to thumping their chests and taking pot shots at the opposition on their 56-inch chest taunts. Post these two game-changing events, these sneers by the opposition stopped. Even if pot shots were taken, they just didn't have the intensity or conviction behind them.

Halfway through his term, Modi had fortified his image of an incorruptible leader. There was not even a single corruption charge against him or his government, which was a huge relief for the people of the country. They were fed up of seeing scams tumbling out of the cupboard of the erstwhile UPA regime, literally on a daily basis during its reign.

Modi had laid down the platform for what would eventually be the most penetrative welfare programme ever for the poor masses of the country. Unfortunately, his welfare strategy always remained below the radar of the Indian media.Their focus seemed to be more on illusions rather than on facts.

Modi had taken the bull by the horns and challenged the Nehruvian order by making the KMG irrelevant, though their ability to hit back was still evident as seen during the intolerance illusion that they conjured up. He was invoking the forgotten real heroes of the Independence struggle and giving them their rightful place. Modi, along with the Swacch Bharat Abhiyaan had also initiated the cleaning up of the economy. There was a sharp focus on internal security and action had been initiated to curb the dangerous Separatist tendencies that threatened the integrity of the country. He had further strengthened his image of a strong and decisive leader. For the first time, India had aggressively responded to Pakistan in its own defence. Nationalism had hit the centre stage. The 56–inch chest was there for all to see!

# Part II
# *Dismantling the Order*

# 7
# The Rise of a Yogi

Year 2017 started on a good note electorally for the BJP. Barring Punjab, where they lost power, they wrested power in or retained all other states that went to polls in 2017. Out of seven such states, they wrested power in five, retained one and lost a coalition government in another. They formed the government in Manipur for the first time ever, confirming that Modi's look east policy was bearing good results. Even though they won less number of seats than the Congress, that also did not have the majority, BJP proved to be lot more agile. It demonstrated political alacrity to form alliances with smaller parties and formed a majority coalition, which was sworn in to form the government. There was a repeat of the same story in Goa.

Rahul Gandhi and Congress party came under a lot of attack for their lazy approach in Goa and Manipur. Congress was dubbed as a party who had lost appetite for a fight and had forgotten how to win. Rahul had led the Congress campaign in 2014 Lok Sabha elections, where the party put up its worst ever performance by winning only 44 seats. Since then, barring Punjab, they lost a string of states. Ironically, despite presiding over all these defeats, the President post of the Congress party was there for Rahul's taking. Media had been speculating Rahul's imminent coronation for a while. However, perhaps he was looking for an opportune moment – a moment of glory, which was not coming – to assume the leadership. Perhaps he was just reluctant. It was matters like these which had earned Rahul the sobriquet of a reluctant politician.

Meanwhile, BJP's victory as well as expansion drive was rolling at full steam. They were utilising technology and social media to the hilt, to grow party membership and claimed to have become the biggest political party in the world. Modi was using every possible channel to connect directly with the people. He was there on mobile, through his app and various social media accounts. He was on the radio through his *Mann ki Baat,* and he would connect with voters directly through scores of rallies that he would conduct during elections, which happened literally throughout the year in India.

However, if perhaps there was one state election that was the most crucial for BJP before the 2019 general elections, it was UP in February 2017. Primarily on two accounts – one, it was pitted as a barometer to gauge the political outcome of demonetisation. BJP's victory would have indicated demonetisation as a huge success, while opposition's victory would have signalled it as an abject failure. Two, UP being the most populous state, which sent 80 Members of Parliament (MPs) to the parliament, it was critical for Modi to win to orchestrate maximum push for welfare schemes and ensure a near repeat performance of 2014 (when they had won 73 seats in UP). It was understood that UP would make or mar BJP prospects in 2019, just as it did in 2014.

The fabled 'man with the Midas touch' as far as political campaigns are concerned – Prashant Kishore – was the poll strategist for Rahul Gandhi for the 2017 UP elections. They kicked off their campaign in September 2016 with '*khat pe chercha*' (discussions on a cot), a series of meetings sitting on a cot, between Rahul and farmers along the stretch of more than two thousand kilometres from Deoria district to Delhi. Rahul clearly seemed to be taking a headstart, kicking off a sure-footed campaign much before any other political party, at least as far as grabbing all the media attention was concerned. However, things went horribly wrong in the very first meeting. What got the most media bites were farmers running away with most of the cots placed at the meeting even before Rahul's *charcha* (discussion) concluded. Sadly, this time around, the media attention was all for the wrong reasons. It is ironic that a campaign to highlight the farmers' plight and distress were leaving the public in splits.

From there on, things only worsened for the Congress. As the campaign went along, in came the news that Priyanka may well be made the campaign in-charge, but that never happened. It ended up as a double whammy. Priyanka not making it would have demoralised the Congress workers while creating a doubt with the public that perhaps Rahul's campaign was not as effective, and he needed reinforcement. Then suddenly, out of nowhere, the news came that Shiela Dixit would be the chief ministerial face of the Congress for UP elections.

While the flip-flops of one 'boy' were on, the other 'boy' was busy in an intriguing battle for the party with his own father. The Yadav family had divided from the middle between the father and the son. Eventually Akhilesh wrested the party hold from

Mulayam and was declared the undisputed head of Samajwadi Party (SP).

Having gained control of the party, this boy met the other boy Rahul, and both decided to team up. Henceforth, throughout the campaign, both would be popularly known as '*UP ke ladke*' (boys of UP) which was the alliance slogan. Akhilesh showed large-heartedness and left an unbelievable 100 seats for Rahul, much to the chagrin of Mulayam. Shiela Dixit became the sacrificial pawn in the larger goal to win UP. It is a known fact that both Akhilesh and Rahul have always had a great personal chemistry and perhaps their assessment was that this great equation amongst the two leaders will pay rich dividends in the dangal (battle) of UP politics.

While all this drama was catching all the media eyeballs, one wandered what was the reason for the complete radio silence at BJP's end. If one was to go by media bytes, it seemed they were yet to launch their UP campaign. However, folks who follow BJP will mention that while most of the other parties manage elections top down, BJP starts from bottom up. Away from the media glare, way back in 2014 after winning the general election, BJP had started the drive for enrolling members across the country and as they did that, their eyes would have especially been on UP elections in 2017. The election booth is their temple and the voter list their bible. They appoint a *panna pramukh* (page head) for every page on the voter list who is required to then connect with all the voters on that page. The page head reports to the booth head and the chain goes right up to the party president, who at that moment was Amit Shah.

As has been reported, Shah checks details right down to the page head to ensure that all bases are covered and it is not just on paper, but actually working on the ground. Shah in many subsequent interviews on TV channels has mentioned how he physically criss-crosses the country right down to the booth level to ensure BJP has an effective, aligned and well-oiled election machine.Very few party presidents would go to such detailing. This exercise can be extremely dull, boring and tedious, which will never attract any media eyeballs, will not attract any publicity and will require people to soil their hands. Even a Member of Legislative Assembly (MLA) may find it beneath him/her to go down to this level. Yet, here was the party president of the world's biggest and India's ruling party, doing exactly that. One needs dollops of internal motivation and drive to do that. So from where do the BJP folks get that? Let us save that question for a little later.

Thus, it was all set in UP. SP-Congress claimed that '*UP ko ladkon ka saath pasand hai*' (UP likes the partnership of the two boys). Mayawati was confident of her unshakable vote bank and Muslim support while BJP was ready with its bow, in the form of its election machinery to shoot its brahmasthra, Modi. Opinion polls before the elections were divided. While one agency gave a slight edge to BJP+, others mostly predicted a hung assembly. However, nobody could have imagined what was about to happen. BJP+ got a whopping 325 seats out of 403, a landslide victory.

What was to happen after this was even more astounding. BJP went into this election without a chief ministerial face. Rumour mills started working overtime and media started speculating various names starting from Rajnath Singh to Varun Gandhi. However, in the end, most of the media reports were veering towards Manoj Sinha – a minister in the Modi government and an MP from Ghazipur, UP at that time – and Keshav Prasad

Maurya, the then BJP-UP President. Finally, it took the wind out of everyone's sails when Yogi Adityanath's name was announced as the new UP Chief Minister.

For the uninitiated, Yogi as CM was a bolt from the blue. However, if one considers the following points, it becomes clear that he was the obvious choice.

BJP's election manifesto had a strong Yogi imprint. Among other key issues, crackdown on slaughterhouses and creating anti-romeo squads found a place of prominence in the manifesto. It was clear that Yogi played an important role in drafting it.

He was one of the key star campaigners of BJP, the only local person among a line-up of national leaders. He was also the most sought-after among BJP candidates for holding rallies in their respective constituencies.

He was by far the most popular local BJP leader in UP. As per media reports, BJP's own internal survey before the elections clearly showed that he was the most popular BJP leader among voters. Even the *India Today*-Axis opinion survey way back in October 2016 projected Yogi as the second best choice as Chief Minister for BJP. Rajnath Singh led the poll by a small margin. It was widely reported that Rajnath Singh was not keen to get back to state politics.

Add to this Yogi's clean and honest image. Plus, had been a five-time parliamentarian. He was also well-versed in running efficient administration being in-charge of his *matha*'s (monastic order) varied interests ranging from hospitals to educational institutions. Though a Rajput, he renounced worldly affairs and assumed the leadership of the Gorakhnath Matha. Maharaj-ji, as he is popularly known, was followed and revered by people from all castes. The fact that the legislators readily accepted him and one heard of no resistance at all points to the fact that he was an appropriate choice.

People, over the period, were most exposed to the Congress culture, and generally had gotten used to a conventional framework of appointment of leaders by the 'high command'. In such a culture, the leader's connectivity and sworn loyalty to the high command were the most critical criterion. BJP, as it did in 2013 when it chose Modi over national stalwarts, by choosing Yogi, yet again was clearly signalling that performance and acceptability on the ground were the most critical criteria for selection of a leader.

Critics were quick to slam Modi for thrusting Hindutva agenda and destroying the secular fabric of our nation. It is true that Yogi's public image is that of a firebrand leader who pushes a hard-core Hindutva agenda. From the media's prism, he was largely viewed as a divisive figure, further reinforced by his sharp repartee to his political opponents during election speeches, i.e. references of Bajrangbali and Ali. However, there is another image of Yogi, which was lesser known and started being reflected only after he became the CM. That too after the media went to Gorakhpur to capture the reaction of people and to get some insights on Yogi's day-to-day life. It turns out that many Muslims came over for his help at his *janta darbar* (public court) which he held regularly. People even said that as soon as he is able to place a Muslim in a crowd, he would attend to him/her first. A Muslim contractor is in charge of all the construction and repair works, including mandirs at his matha, and has free access to all places. Many Muslims run shops within the matha's compound and many other depend for their livelihood on the ashram. There are stories of how Yogi sorted issues of beleaguered Muslims whose lands were grabbed.

So how does one reconcile these vastly contrasting images of Yogi? On the one hand, he is a hardliner who fights for Hindu *asmita* (pride), and on the other hand, he is a humanitarian who goes out of the way to help people, irrespective of their faiths. Why is it that he is such a completely different person on stage than he is when his feet are on the ground? One gets some clues in Shatanu Gupta's book on Yogi. He mentions that the issue of religious oppression and persecution during the medieval period was close to Yogi's heart. He goes on to state that Yogi was incensed with Congress and other regional parties for adopting a formula of appeasing Muslims while keeping Hindus divided by castes for electoral gains. It seems, Yogi's angst is squarely directed towards the Congress and opposition parties that are, in his understanding, the key reasons for dividing the country by playing vote bank politics of caste, creed, religion, etc.

He seems to have finally discovered a trick to neutralise that formula. His elation was amply evident when in the parliament while giving his farewell speech, he said to Mr Kharge, the then leader of opposition from Congress party in the Lok Sabha – "I am younger to Rahul ji by one year and elder to Akhilesh Yadav by one year. Since I came in between the pair, I feel, that is one of the key reasons for your failure." The house erupted in laughter.

Yogi had indeed broken the backbone of Rahul-Akhilesh partnership and set the stage for 2019. Yogi had struck hard to dismantle the caste divide and a key aspect of the Nehruvian order, a manufactured myth.

# 8
# Motivated Election Machine

Standing in the middle of the battlefield, Arjun gazed at his enemy on the opposite side. He saw his brothers, the Kauravas; his guru, Dronacharya; and the one whom he loved and revered the most, Bhishma. He lost all will and energy to fight, his shoulders drooped, his bow dropped from his hands and he fell on his knees, dejected and crestfallen. "I cannot kill my own," he pleaded. What followed was a divine lesson by Krishna, eventually immortalised in Gita, a holy scripture, which has acted like a moral compass and spiritual guide for generation after generation.

"This is a war of dharma (right principles), a righteous war which you have to win for the betterment of this world and for generations to come; and only you can demolish the evil on the other side", advised Krishna. Krishna made Arjun aware of the higher purpose, which was not to kill his relatives but to establish dharma. The higher purpose awakened Arjun's higher consciousness, sparked a surge of energy in his being and the rest, as we all know, is history.

Closer to our times, reputed corporations across the globe have realised the importance of invoking a higher purpose of their organisation to align and motivate their employees to deliver peak performance. In late 1980s, we witnessed an immensely popular advertisement from Tata Steel whose tagline went, "We also make steel". Well, in effect, they only made steel. However, they were publicly expressing their higher purpose, which they had invoked in their employees to align and motivate them to achieve their corporate goals.

Ever wondered why a soldier is motivated to give his/her life in the battlefield? Will he/she give up life if he/she was told that the purpose was to merely kill as many soldiers as possible on the other side? They do it because they believe that their country is fighting for a just cause, which needs to be upheld, come what may. They do it to protect their fellow soldiers and they do it for the pride of their regiment. It is this higher purpose that makes them sacrifice their lives happily.

Now we come back to the point raised earlier in the book on BJP's drive to work relentlessly, round the clock, as a well-oiled election machine, going right down to the level of panna pramukh and connecting with voters, page by page covering the length and breadth of the country, facing all the hardships of travel, inclement weather, inaccessibility, and in many cases, facing the ire of voters. This is such a thankless, boring, tedious job and yet BJP workers do it day in day out, irrespective of whether there is an election or not. The answer is simple, a higher purpose, which is to make India great again. To be a Vishwa guru. And how does one do that? By making the country strong and by uplifting its people and making them strong, the principle propounded by its founder Deen Dayal Upadhyay, popularly known as *Antyodaya* (upliftment of the weakest section of the society). To further motivate its forces, they liberally invoke the past glory of India and use that as a backdrop to build a vision for the future.

For this purpose, they draw inspiration from RSS, which acts as a moral guide to the BJP. Their strident Hindu stance aside, though which does appear to be becoming more and more inclusive with changing times, RSS commitment to the nation and its people is unquestionable. Their commitment to social and economic betterment of the citizens of India and working selflessly towards that goal is for all to see. BJP has adopted these values from the RSS and a seamless flow of folks from RSS to BJP and vice-versa keeps up the momentum.

Lutyen's media and Khan Market Gang are quick to target BJP. They point out this relentless, selfless zeal of its cadres and discredit it by calling it a rabid force borne out of hatred. They decry that to keep their cadre pumped-up, BJP ends up creating an imaginary enemy all the time. They claim this was the key reason why Pakistan has become a flash point with India as BJP has been targeting it unnecessarily. They allege Modi's belligerent reaction to Pakistan was one of the key reasons why he won 2014 general elections, which is why they state, he continues with the same muscular policy for his selfish political gains. However, in 2014, the facts bore out something else.

Leading up to the 2014 elections, we were in a situation where terrorists were exploding bombs across the country, killing scores of innocent people. It was a time when people were scared of going to crowded places or malls fearing for their lives. Mumbai attacks were still fresh in people's minds, also because of the helplessness shown by the then Manmohan Singh government and its pusillanimous response. The nation was impatient and crying for a strong and decisive leader. Nature abhors vacuum and in stepped Narendra Modi. Modi did not create or imagine that situation. It was the situation which created the space for Modi.

People saw this as a challenge and thought Modi to be the most capable person to have overcome the grave situation. Hence, they catapulted him into the top leadership role of the country.

Of course, political parties can drum up issues and create a charade, but if it does not resonate with people, it will never last long. And, no issue, unless it is real, will ever resonate with people for long. The Lutyen's media and KMG were desperately trying to create a false notion that BJP's ascent was based on manufactured imaginary issues and not real ones, whether they would be able to cast a spell on the public's mind on this? They did not succeed in 2014. Only time would tell if they meet with some success in 2019.

Hence, the key point to understand in the 2014 BJP victory is that BJP cadres were motivated by a higher purpose that drives them as well as resonates with people, and they further got a boost by the vacuum created in the external environment that was seeking a leader like Modi. These two factors acted as a double engine that propelled Modi to Prime Ministership.

The only other party that could boast of such a motivated and committed cadre would be the communists. They too are devoted to their chosen cause. However, that cadre base was shrinking fast and the signs were ominous for them with the Congress making it even worse by appropriating that shrinking base. Why may that be happening, though? Why was a motivated and committed cadre base of Communists shrinking? Perhaps it was time for them to ask an existential question, "Why do we exist"?

Since we are at it, what would be the higher purpose or cause of the Congress party? Both these questions will be answered later in the book.

# 9
# Hindi-Chini Bhai Bhai!!

"Rubbish, total rubbish! We do not need a defence policy. Our policy is *ahimsa* (non-violence). We foresee no military threats. As far as I am concerned, you can scrap the army, the police are good enough to meet our security needs," said Nehru to the then commander in chief of the Indian army, General Sir Rob Lockhart. This was around the time after India gained independence, when he went to meet Nehru on the defence policy.

There is a popular folklore on Hanuman while he was still a kid. His legendary strength was already obvious. A sage called Matang muni got annoyed with his pranks demonstrating his extraordinary powers and cursed him that he shall forget all his strength and magical powers. However, foreseeing the future, he also added that in times of genuine need, when reminded, his strength will return to him.

In the twentieth century, Nehru turned out to be Matang muni for the Indian army. Only he could never foresee the future and lessen his curse. There are enough instances documented which point to Nehru's deep suspicion of Indian defence forces as well as its futility. Ex-Army Chief General J.N. Chaudhari at a lecture in Cambridge in 1973 said, "The first fifteen years after Independence were lean ones for India's armed forces. Budget allotments were restricted, provisions for new equipment was slow, and in the case of Indian Navy, almost non-existent. There was no firm decision as to what the ultimate strength of the armed forces should be. This had its effect on morale…." He goes on to say later in the same lecture, "From time to time, the Prime Minister (Nehru) took on the defence portfolio, but being a very busy man, could only deal with in a somewhat desultory way. It appears to us that he did not visualise a serious defence problem arising…"

In 1950, when we were still fighting a proxy war with Pakistan, and China had moved into Tibet, the Indian army strength was reduced by fifty thousand men. There was another proposal to reduce the size of men by another one lakh in 1951, but it was not implemented. Nehru was so driven by his ideology of non-alignment and disarmament that he refused to recognise any external threats. In all fairness, no one can blame Nehru for having such lofty ideals, but his insistence to actualise those ideals in total disregard of the ground situation and against numerous advices given to him by top Indian Army leadership is just astonishing. It has been well documented that the then Defence Minister, Krishna Menon, Nehru's kindred, tried to politicise army by creating a rift between the then Army Chief Gen. Thimayya and his number two, Gen. Thapar.

This approach led Nehru from one blunder to another, severely compromising India's internal as well as external security. His delusional world view made him offer Tibet and UN permanent Security Council seat to China on a platter. The wounds of Kashmir continue to fester until today. His blind trust in China, which made the term "Hindi-Chini Bhai Bhai"

(India and China are brothers) so famous, led India to a most humiliating defeat in 1962 and made us realise how badly he had misread the whole situation. In fact, the term 'Himalayan blunder' would prove to be too small for Nehru's follies. Hence, a blunder even bigger than the Himalayan blunder, should perhaps most appropriately be credited to his name, i.e. Nehruvian blunder!

The KMG will quickly pounce on this and ask why we need to bring Nehru in all discussions. Well, this is a good question and there are two key reasons for it. One is that to solve any problem, you do need to get to the root of it. Unfortunately, the most complex problems that India faces – like Kashmir and by extension Pakistan, China, etc. – go back to Nehru. Secondly, and very importantly, Congress continues to follow the same doctrines adopted by Nehru during his regime. Indeed, even now, Congress itself never tires up talking about Nehru, glowingly attributing their party's doctrines, strategies, policies and programmes to his legacy.

The moot point to understand here is that today's Congress continues to be living in a time warp, still harping on the redundant doctrines of the past. Just to highlight this point, among others, there were three key decisive moments in recent times, which the country faced and Congress failed India while following the anachronistic Nehruvian doctrine of disarmament and peaceful co-existence.

First were the nuclear tests. Rao, Vajpayee's predecessor told him after the tests were conducted, perhaps jokingly, the bombs were already ready, and you just exploded them. Rao had buckled under international pressure and aborted the programme during his regime.

Second was the more recent, Anti Satellite Missile System, which India tested in the first quarter of 2019, which made it only the fourth nation, after US, Russia and China, to successfully conduct the test. We had the capability to conduct the same tests in 2012-13, but sadly, the approval never came from the UPA government.

Third were the Mumbai attacks. The spectacular nature of the attacks in November 2008 stood out even more so starkly against a very meek response by the then Indian government. The attack that continued for days in full public view, globally, shook and agitated the whole nation. The inadequacy of the response led to dejection and disillusionment.

While Nehru left, Matang muni remained in the Congress regime until recent past.

It is in this backdrop that the Doklam issue has to be viewed. Given India's passive cum diffident approach to China thus far, the face off was a watershed moment in India's security and foreign policy. Doklam is a disputed area between Bhutan and China. It is a tri-junction having boundary with India too. India does not claim Doklam but supports Bhutan's claim on it. In June 2017, China started extending a road from their side of the border into Doklam. Indian troops entered the area and thwarted the attempt, leading to a stand-off between the two nations. This face-off continued until August 2017 and the situation finally was de-escalated through diplomatic efforts. Both sides agreed to retract to their earlier positions.

This was a bold move against China, not to protect India's own territory, but that of a friendly neighbour, Bhutan. Compare this incident with China's annexation of Tibet, which India meekly accepted, and the difference is stark. This showed Modi government's resolve, marking a clear shift towards a more muscular security policy and attracted many eyeballs globally. To the larger world, it sent a clear signal that India was ready to take on the hegemonic tendencies of the regional power.

There was another reason why this incident attracted many eyeballs within the country. In the midst of this standoff, when things were heating up and even a war was no longer an improbable consequence, out came the news that Rahul Gandhi had a meeting with the Chinese ambassador. After initial dithering, Congress finally owned up and admitted to the meeting, however, claimed it was only a courtesy call. Only Rahul and Congress would know the real reasons, but to meet an ambassador of a country with whom you are on a brink of war without even informing the government of the day, is highly inappropriate and bound to draw a lot of suspicion. It was extremely bad optics for Congress and Rahul, to say the least, and rightly came under a lot of criticism by public at large. It was Rahul's Jai Chand/Mir Jafar moment!

It reminded one of another Jai Chand/Mir Jafar moment, this time with Pakistan, when Mani Shankar Aiyar, a senior Congressman, in November 2015, in a TV studio debate in Pakistan on how to break Indo-Pak impasse, openly remarked, "*Hamein le aiiye, inko (Modi) hataiiye*" (Bring us, remove Modi). The Pakistani hosts were thoroughly amused and the anchor had to seek a clarification saying, "*Aap ISI se keh rahe hein, ya kis se keh rahe hein? Aap ne nikalna hai*" (Are you telling this to ISI? Who are you telling this? You are the one who has to remove him).

Modi kept on hitting the right notes with his muscular foreign policy, surgical strikes, Doklam, anti-satellite missile, etc., while Congress and the opposition kept of hitting self-goals by sometimes playing a Matang Muni, or a Jai Chand or a Mir Jafar!

Nehruvian doctrines were being dismantled and given burials one by one, and each time it happened, it is only fair to invoke Nehru. Modi was breaking away from the past and heralding a New India which was bold, fearless, strong and resolute. It understood the dreams of the aspirational India, instilling a sense of immense national pride as well as hope.

On the other hand, Amit Shah had set a goal of 350+ seats for BJP in 2019 general elections. They had identified 150 seats to focus on, which they had lost in 2014, but had stood second or a close third. Even for a staunch Modi supporter, it looked a bit too ambitious. However, Modi and Amit Shah were known to take bold, fearless and stretched targets, in line with the traits of a 'New India'.

# 10
# The Illusionists Strike Again

As Modi had successfully started destroying the Nehruvian order bit-by-bit, three plus years into his term, the KMG and Lutyen's media were perhaps seething with anger from inside while replenishing their war chest, ready to attack Modi again, when some help came from unexpected quarters.

Mayawati, post-2017 UP Election defeat, raised serious allegations in a press conference about EVMs (Electronic Voting Machines) having been compromised. Without sharing any shred of proof, she made some outlandish claims that either the machines were manipulated in a way that only BJP votes were being registered or most of the non-BJP votes were going into BJP's account. Congress was quick to take it up from where Mayawati left, and raised a huge clamour, blaming the Modi government for EVM tampering. Joint press conferences of the opposition were held on the issue, representations were made to the Election Commission. From then on, there were demands made of going back to the manual voting system. In hindsight, it seemed the purpose for raising this was two-fold. One obvious reason looked to be to create doubts in the mind of the public and discredit Modi and BJP's electoral victories. The second underlying reason appeared to be to use this issue as a rallying point for opposition unity.

Anti-Modi narrative looked to have several strands. One was to paint BJP as a Hindu Nationalist party, which was intolerant to diversity. The other appeared to project Modi as an authoritarian who was hell bent on compromising the constitutional institutions. The third was to try to destroy Modi's personal incorruptible image. Eventually, the idea seemed to be to create an impression that a corrupt Modi had dictatorial tendencies running a fascist regime. EVM issue fitted in very well with that narrative and the controversy was kept boiling right until the 2019 general elections.

The other two notable controversies, which grabbed media attention around the time of the EVM issue were the allegations against Amit Shah's son, Jay Shah, as well as the Judge Loya controversy. Generally, there was a pattern as to how these controversies were raked. An anti-BJP news portal, known for eye-catching sensational news, publishes a story, as well as goes about whining how the mainstream national news channels will not raise it because of the fear of Modi government. The Congress would be quick to pick them up and subsequently, the national media would splash it all over.

Jay Shah's case was interesting and it seemed to be an attempt to destroy Modi's clean image. The fact that Modi did not have a family had further bolstered his image. In India, generally people toil, work hard acquire wealth largely to better the lives of their children and future generations. Therefore, the way the logic worked in people's mind was that since Modi did not have a family, hence he did not have to bequeath anything to anyone, so he had no desire for materialistic acquisitions and pursuits. To counter that, apparently, the attempt was to create an impression that he was unduly helping his close associates. Earlier, a similar ploy had not worked with the 'suit boot ki sarkar' allegations. This seemed to be another serious attempt to besmirch Modi's clean image, as Amit Shah was perceived to be someone extremely close to Modi. So the hope would have been that the optics being created would hit home.

Both the stories were beautifully scripted. However, they missed one minor detail – the proof. They would extract a fig leaf out of somewhere and build it up through spectacular speculations and assumptions, leaving the accused with the onerous task of proving himself not guilty. The objective perhaps was not so much to prove the guilt, but to give talking points to the Congress against Modi, which would eventually become the fulcrum on which the opposition would weave its narrative.

As far as these two cases are concerned, eventually the Supreme Court summarily dismissed Judge Loya's case. It was claimed that the judge did not die a natural death, but a conspiracy was hatched and he was murdered, as he was the judge in a case against Amit Shah. The Supreme Court rejected that claim.

In the Jay Shah case, Jay filed a defamation case against the news website, which alleged that Jay Shah's business had grown exponentially since Modi became the PM, insinuating that the government granted undue favours to Jay Shah. The website went to the Supreme Court against the Gujarat High Court order in the defamation case filed by Jay. The website eventually withdrew its appeal from Supreme Court, but not before the apex court expressed anguish over the way journalism was being practised in the country.

In early June 2017, NDTV was raided by CBI, which had registered a case against them for having allegedly caused a loss of forty-eight crore rupees to a private bank. These raids triggered an avalanche of criticism against the Modi government. Reports claimed that Modi had waged a war against the media and against press freedom. The opposition quickly pounced on this and alleged that Modi was trying to muzzle the press and was using strong-arm tactics with those channels who refused to fall in line with him.

In January 2018, something completely unexpected and unprecedented happened. Four senior Supreme Court judges had an open press conference informing the nation of the challenges the Apex Court was facing. The key issue was the way the allocation of cases was happening and the demand was that that there should be a clearly laid down objective criteria for the same. When the stunned media contingent asked them whether they had broken ranks, Justice Ranjan Gogoi, who eventually succeeded Justice Dipak Misra as the Chief Justice of India said, "Nobody is breaking the rank; it's a discharge of debt to the nation which we have done."

This conference was to eventually take a political hue, when after the conference Justice Chelameswar, who was one of the four judges conducting the press conference, was spotted shaking hands with D. Raja, Communist Party of India leader at his own residence. Later D. Raja clarified that it was a personal meeting, but his party disapproved of him meeting Justice Chelameswar.

Congress party was again quick to jump into the fray and alleged that it was another example of how the Modi government was meddling in the democratic institutions. The insinuation was that the then Chief Justice Dipak Misra was hand-in-glove with the government and together they were managing allocation of crucial cases to pliable judges. To raise the crescendo, the opposition led by Congress submitted a petition for the impeachment of Chief Justice Dipak Misra to the Vice President, which he eventually rejected.

Raking up of these controversies also seemed to be a clever attempt to put a negative spin to the strong image of Modi. They alleged that he was using his brute strength to muzzle the press, misuse institutions like CBI and Enforcement Directorate to force his opponents to fall in line, subvert the courts, make Election Commission pliable and unethically help his close associates to amass wealth. They claimed that Modi was misusing his strengths by exploiting the whole government machinery at his command, to destroy the democratic institutions and taking the country towards dictatorship.

Not for no reason, there were several attempts made to equate Modi to Hitler. It seemed the objective was to communicate to the public at large that even Hitler was strong but on the evil side. And so was our man - Modi. It looked like a good plan, but the key was to back their narrative with substantive proofs, otherwise it would just be akin to creating an illusion yet again, which would get broken in no time or have no real impact on the public.

Three years plus into the Modi term, Congress seemed to be pulling its act together and sharpening its attack on the government around these controversies. They definitely were quickest off the block in picking up these issues and running with them. Lutyen's media would ensure that Congress hogged the limelight on these issues for a fair length of time, while never ever looking at the veracity of the allegations. It appeared that Congress was getting more than adequate support from the

KMG. Congress seemed to be looking to drive the anti-Modi narrative that resonated with all opposition parties, which could then act as glue, enabling it to become the party around whom all other opposition parties would rally around, making it the natural claimant to lead the eventual grand 'Mahagathbandhan'.

Congress had another ace up its sleeve. Rahul had put the Rafale jet in motion and it was already airborne for Gujarat.

# 11
# The 'myth' of Being Secular

"Secularism is indifference or rejection or exclusion of religions or religious consideration." – *Merriam-Webster* dictionary.

"Secularism is the belief that religion should not be involved with the ordinary social and political activities of a country." – *Collins* dictionary.

The campaigning for Gujarat state elections in Nov-Dec 2017 had begun and Rahul's new avatar as a Shiv *bhakt* and *janeu dhari* was being unveiled gradually. Rahul was temple hopping at a feverish pace throughout Gujarat. His temple visits were getting far more coverage in the media than what he said at the rallies and you would not be able to blame anyone if one was to get the impression that the divine visits seemed to be the main agenda and election rallies just happened on the way from one temple to the other. If it was *khat pe chercha* in UP, it seemed it was *Mandir mein bhakti* (prayer in the temple) this time in Gujarat.

Sonia Gandhi defended Rahul's temple hopping by saying that BJP had managed to convince people that the Congress is a Muslim party. And because it was pushed into a corner, rather than going to the temples quietly, little more of public focus has been put on it. It was a very matter of fact kind of response, and sadly, there was no counter-question to her on that by the interviewer. The fact was that they were compromising on secularism, yet again. Anyway, Rahul would later actually go on to contradict his mother and say that Congress is a Muslim party as claimed by an Urdu daily *Inquilab*. Congress never contested that daily on it. It is amazing how Congress plays the communal card so brazenly and yet they are never questioned on it, leave aside being labelled as communal. Ever wondered why?

During Madhya Pradesh (MP) state elections, Kamal Nath in an election meeting was seen on camera, saying, "*Agar musalmaan ke 90 percent vote nahi padhe to haemin bahut badaa nuksaan ho sakta hai.*" (If 90% Muslims will not vote, it can result in a big loss for us). I wonder why Kamal Nath was never labelled as communal. Moreover, if as a reaction to such statements, Yogi Adityanath says, that if they have Ali, we have Bajrangbali, why is he viciously attacked and the world is reminded of his strident communal side? Just like Sonia Gandhi, why was the matter not put to rest when Yogi responded that he said it only when he was pushed to a corner? Why is Rahul not communal when he says that Congress is a party for Muslims, but Yogi is communal when he says that Bajrangbali is with us?

If we go back a few years when the then Prime Minister, Manmohan Singh stated in a formal meeting as a matter of government's policy intent that "Muslims should have a first right to the country's resources," why wasn't Manmohan Singh as well as Congress stamped as communal?

Going back further to 1986, when the then PM Rajiv Gandhi passed a bill in the parliament undoing the Supreme Court verdict in Shah Bano case, ostensibly to please the Muslim clergy. Then, perhaps with a view to please the Hindus, he quickly went on to have the gates of Ram Mandir at the Babri Masjid site opened and subsequently, presided over the Shilanyas. That triggered a sequence of events, which culminated with L.K. Advani's *rath yatra*, building a huge momentum for the BJP. The irony is that L.K. Advani and BJP were labelled as communal and Rajiv came out squeaky clean. Then again, during the 1984 Sikh pogrom, post Indira Gandhi's assassination, Rajiv Gandhi responded by saying that when a big tree falls, earth is bound to shake.

So what is it that makes the Gandhis and the Congress party so immune to the "communal" label?

We find the answer in Dr Yuval Noah Harari's international bestseller, *Sapiens*. He says humans are the only living beings who have the capability to imagine. He further writes in his book, "Homo sapiens can speak about things that don't really exist, and believe six impossible things before breakfast. You could never convince a monkey to give you a banana by promising him limitless bananas after death in monkey-heaven. Fiction has enabled us not merely to imagine things, but to do so collectively. We can weave common myths."

A myth is an idea or a concept, which may or may not have a basis, but if it goes unchallenged over a long enough period, people eventually start accepting it.

History tells us that man has been creating myths since time immemorial; sometimes for the good of man, sometimes for vested interests. There are numerous examples where myths were created to prop up a monarch and to ensure his dynasty's longevity. Timur Lang was known for his ruthlessness. When he defeated the King Bayezid of the Ottoman Empire, after brutally devastating his army, his court historians were concerned that people may fear his brutality and not accept him. Hence, they gave him a title of Sahib Kiran (a just world conqueror, whose generations will rule) to inspire awe. At the same time, by calling him a just ruler, gain immediate respect and acceptability from the people of that empire.

So also, titles like 'the great', 'Alam Panah', 'Jahan Panah', before a king's or emperor's real name had exactly the same purpose. The king was addressed by his title and not the name, so his manufactured greatness was reinforced repeatedly. Over time, people would start imagining that the king, indeed, possessed the qualities reflected in the title. These were myths created to draw allegiance of the people whom the king ruled over.

So also, in independent and modern India too, a myth was created that the Indian National Congress was the synonym for secularism and the Nehru Gandhi dynasty, by virtue of being the rightful heirs of Mahatma Gandhi after having adopting his surname, had also assumed from the Mahatma the role of being the paragons of secularism in India. Hence, irrespective of howsoever they may behave and act, they would always be the exemplars of secularism in India. We, like our medieval ancestors, fell for that myth.

This is not all. To further bolster the myth, the word 'secularism' is defined neither in our Constitution, nor in our laws. Hence that role to define it fell conveniently in the lap of the propaganda machine, Lutyen's media. Ably representing the dynasty, they would deftly define secularism using complex terms and words. Having thoroughly confused the gullible citizenry, Lutyen's media would add nuances to tweak the meaning depending on the shifts in the opportunistic dynasty's take on secularism from time to time. Ironically, all these definitions were not even close to the dictionary meaning, or the way it was practised in the western world, where this word originated.

We, the people, would continue to be in awe of the articulate play of words and readily accept whatever was placed before us in the name of secularism. The KMG and Lutyen's media drilled this myth in our heads for decades, so our brains would suddenly freeze when we heard the word 'secularism' and look up to the Congress, Gandhis, KMG and the Lutyen's media for direction. It was as if a spell had been cast on the citizens. Since the Indian state had complete control on media and communication until early 2000s, the KMG and Lutyen's media had it easy. It was only when media started becoming privatised and channels like Times Now, Republic, India Today, CNN, ABP, Aaj Tak, India TV and scores of others gradually started challenging this myth that our eyes seem to be opening up, though we still are far off from complete enlightenment.

BJP has been the chief whipping boy for Congress when it comes to secularism. Within BJP, people like Yogi Adityanath are the easy targets, who have become the poster boys for Congress to fear-monger and have been labelled as the mascots of Hindu radicalism, by the KMG and Lutyen's media. Yogi's 'Ali vs Bajrangbali' remark in the 2019 general elections got a lot of press and was claimed as a proof of his radical views. He had made that comment in a rally at Meerut in April 2019 in response to a direct call of Mayawati to Muslims to vote for her. However, it was not the first time Yogi had made that comment. He had made that comment first time in MP state elections in response to the "90 percent Muslim vote…" comment by Kamal

Nath. It is ironic that while the press forgot about Kamal Nath's and Mayawati's comments, Yogi's comment continues to make circulation in the media. This is how myths are manufactured.

However, the key point in Yogi's speech is that it shows his angst against the Congress and is directly an outcome of the appeasement politics under the garb of secularism. Rather than reconciling the pain of oppression by past regimes, the wounds have gone deeper and people like Yogi manifest that. It also has to be acknowledged and recognised that people like Yogi actually represent the sentiments of millions of Indians. That's why Yogi is BJP's one of the top two or three star campaigners who is most in demand. His presence elicits huge crowds and people respond to him with great gusto, and his appeal is only growing.

If someone were to ask the question, "Why is Yogi so angry?" The answer simply would be the myth of secularism manufactured by the KMG. While the neutral and so-called nationalist TV News channels have slowly started chipping away on this myth of secularism in the cosy confines of their newsrooms among their intellectual panellists, on the ground, Yogi has launched a frontal attack and is hammering this myth hard, determined to break it into smithereens. Lutyen's media can keep shouting from their rooftops that Yogi is a polarising figure, but the fact of the matter is that he is attacking the duplicity of Congress and its appeasement politics, and he is resonating with the people. Yogi's crusade is well on its way.

Coming back to the Congress, Gandhis and Gujarat, though they lost the state, they gave a good fight to the BJP. However, the KMG was at it again and hailed it as a moral victory for Congress. It seemed like this time, Congressmen completely fell for this myth, as one could see it on their faces. They had spring in their steps and belief in their eyes.

Congress's moral victory reminded us of a popular Bollywood movie dialogue, *"Haar ker jitney wale ko baazigar kehte hein"* (One who wins even after losing is called a magician). Rahul had become the President of India National Congress, taking over from his mother, just a couple of days before the Gujarat election results were declared. While Congress had lost, Rahul had to be somehow shown as a winner to justify Rahul's accession. Since he led the Gujarat campaign, Congress had to be projected as triumphant. Hence, the term moral victory.

Newspapers were full of reports on how Rahul had shown spunk and given a real fight to Modi. Media claimed that Rahul had finally put his act together and Congress ascendance had started! The spell had been cast, yet again! Lutyen's media had yet again proved that they indeed were magicians, illusionists par excellence.

# 12
# A Blessing in Disguise

*Phullan da tu attar banaa* (make perfume from flowers)
*Attran da fir kadd dariya* (make so much that a river of perfume flows)
*Dariya vich fir rajj ke naha* (bathe in that river to your heart's content)
*Macchiyan wangu tariya la* (swim and dive like a fish in it)
*Fer vi teri bo nahi mukkni* (even then your foul body odour will not go)
*Pehlan apni mein muka.* (For that you first need to get rid of your ego)

— *Bulleh Shah, a Punjabi Sufi poet (1680-1757)*

2018 was not a good year for the BJP, though they began the year well, winning all three Northeast states that went to poll in February-March. Tripura called for a special mention where BJP formed the state government on its own, going from zero to thirty-six seats and the vote percentage went up from 1.5% to 43%. It was an unprecedented result for the party as Tripura was considered a red bastion where CPI(M) was in power for twenty-five years continuously prior to these elections. NDA also won Meghalaya and Nagaland.

Mahagathbandhan seemed to have started taking baby steps. The unthinkable had happened in UP. Bua-bhatija (Mayawati and Akhilesh) had come together for the by-polls to be held in three UP constituencies – Phulpur, Kairana and the prestigious seat of Yogi Adityanath, Gorakhpur. Mayawati had decided to support SP in all these three seats. It was in all probability an experiment, as they wanted to see if the votes would transfer. The experiment was successful and SP won all the three seats, much to the disappointment of BJP, but a huge morale boost for the opposition. The opposition had tasted blood and claimed that BJP's *acchhe din* (good days) were over. While Akhilesh termed it as "popular anger" against BJP, Mamta Banerjee tweeted, "The beginning of the end has started." Around a year away from general elections, it was clearly bad optics for BJP.

The first semi-final was in Karnataka where Congress was in government. The highest number of seats was won by BJP but it fell a few seats short of majority. They tried to form the government, but lost the trust vote, which eventually led to an alliance between Congress and Janta Dal (Secular) (JDS) that finally formed the government with K.D. Kumaraswamy of JDS as the chief minister. It was clearly another setback for BJP but the opposition again got a chance to be jubilant. At Kumaraswamy's oath-taking ceremony, it was perhaps only the second time after demonetisation that the whole opposition was together in a single screen shot. It was a great photo op for the opposition to show their bonhomie, sometimes hugging each other, sometimes holding hands and waving to the crowd. The KMG must have been grinning from ear to ear. The pieces of the puzzle seemed to be falling into place; the narrative looked like working with the people and the right atmospherics were developing for the final assault to bleed Modi with 543 cuts.

They would have been hoping for the final impetus to come from the second semi-final in Rajasthan, Chhattisgarh and Madhya Pradesh later on at the end of 2018. Their hopes were indeed realised. On 11 December 2018, after winning the three Hindi heartland states of Rajasthan, Gujarat and Chhattisgarh, Rahul Gandhi did a press conference in which he said a few things, which viewed in hindsight reveal a lot about him as a person. Rahul said that the 2014 general elections were the best thing that happened to him as he learnt a lot through it. He claimed that he learnt humility, he learnt that it was important to listen to what the people of the country felt. He went on to say in that context that he learnt a lot from Modi, of how you should *not* do things. He said Modi had a huge opportunity in 2014 but the sad thing was, and he felt bad for Modi, for he refused to listen to the youth and the farmers. Rahul concluded by saying that a certain amount of arrogance had come in Modi which, he thought, was fatal for a politician.

Rahul appeared to be already talking about Modi in the past tense. It seemed, post this victory, he was convinced in his mind that it was the end of the road for Modi and his game was over. He seemed to have missed a few key undercurrents, some obvious and some not so obvious. For example, in Rajasthan, during the elections, one was hearing a common refrain from people all across the state, "Modi *tujh se bair nahi,* Vasundhra *teri khair nahi* (Nothing against Modi, but Vasundhara has had it!). Of all the sloganeering from both parties, this was perhaps the most widespread across Rajasthan. Then we had the opinion polls telling us that there was no anti-incumbency against Modi. People now were discerning enough to view state and central elections separately. Come central elections, and the voting patterns, in all probability, were going to change.

However, Rahul as well as the Congress seemed so blinded by their smugness and overconfidence that either they could genuinely not see the signs or were in a denial. What was to follow their victories in Rajasthan and MP were bad optics, especially in a democracy and reminded people, once again, the monarchic traits of the Congress. The Congress high command culture was in full display as the jostling for chief minister's post had started in both states. Ashok Gehlot and Sachin Pilot from Rajasthan as well as Kamal Nath and Jyotiraditya Scindia from MP started a series of visits to Sonia and Rahul's residences. To heighten the royal effect, Priyanka too joined in. It seemed hectic negotiations were going on; big egos were being bruised and placated. Watching on television sets, an ordinary viewer would have felt as if he was watching a drama on palace intrigues, enacted by the Czar and his chieftains. The key features of a monarchy were on full display, in a vibrant democracy.

News reports were saying that while the youngsters were perhaps the better choice, an expedient call was made to go with seniors as they were better placed to deliver in general elections 2019. In today's day and age, that seemed a bizarre argument. One would assume that a better choice would deliver better results at the state and hence improve your probability of success in 2019? The political analysts and KMG would argue that it is about *jod-tod*, *jugaad* and money. They forget that before any of that, it is about performance and delivery. It is amazing how a section of political experts would be so out of touch with the lexicon of New India. Contrast that with UP and how Yogi was chosen, and the difference is obvious. On one side was performance and on the other side were loyalty, jod-tod, jugaad and money!

The BJP surely must have got a jolt by the results of these semi-finals. That perhaps triggered the urgency in them and they moved quickly to seal their alliances for 2019. Moreover, also because they had lost a big ally, Telugu Desam Party (TDP), ostensibly for not agreeing to grant special status to Andhra Pradesh while the reports suggested that it was probably because of local compulsions. The state elections were approaching and an anti-centre stand would boost their chances to win. However, leaving NDA could not save Chandrababu Naidu from losing.

As per media reports, it seemed there were particularly two partners where BJP may face complications. There were unconfirmed reports that Nitish Kumar from Bihar may be looking for other options. Amit Shah quickly moved in and closed the deal. BJP-JDU (Janata Dal United) would fight seventeen seats each while six were left for Ram Vilas Paswan's Lok Janshakti Party (LJP). That was quite a surprise as generally there was an expectation that BJP would fight higher number of seats than the JDU.

Shiv Sena and BJP had really been an intriguing partnership. Ideologically they make a good couple, but Shiv Sena was by far BJP's most vocal critic, perhaps even more so than the opposition parties were, while Shiv Sena continued to be in the government. Not a day would pass when *Saamna* (Shiv Sena's publication) would not be criticising some aspect or the other of the Modi government. Hence, the concern was that this time, it would be tough for BJP to strike a deal with Shiv Sena. However, it raised quite a few eyebrows when Amit Shah signed a 50-50 deal with Shiv Sena for the Lok Sabha elections. No one expected that the BJP would give in so much. It seemed like the loss in Rajasthan, MP and Chattisgarh had pushed BJP to move in, close the deals quickly and obviate any further setback, even if it meant that they needed to be more accommodating and flexible. In hindsight, the losses perhaps turned out to be a good providence for the BJP.

On the other hand, Congress had a huge opportunity. By all accounts, 2018 was an excellent year for them. They had the momentum with them and the three state victories in December, just months before the general elections, had given a huge impetus not just to the Congress party, but also to the whole opposition. Congress had seemingly been setting a strong narrative while the whole opposition was rallying around them and now it was for the Congress to seize the initiative. They had to be the glue for the Mahagathbandhan.

Most of the opposition was keen on an anti-Modi Mahagathbandhan, and there were three people who seemed to be making some efforts towards it. The first one was K. Chandrashekhar Rao, the CM of Telengana. Soon after winning the state, he initiated efforts towards forming a third front. His aim was to have an anti-BJP and anti-Congress front and he started talking to all the key players. Reports suggested that he had national ambitions and wanted to leave the state for his son. The big catch though with him was that he was looking for not just an anti-Modi front, but also an anti-Congress front. His efforts were geared towards a front equidistant from both the BJP as well as the Congress.

The second person making efforts was Chandrababu Naidu of TDP from Andhra Pradesh. Having been the convener of

NDA1, the first successful coalition under the leadership of Vajpayee, he perhaps had the capability to stitch a multi-party alliance. Unfortunately, after his loss in state elections, he had lost the stature required for such an onerous task. However, he probably was the least ambitious of the three and did look genuinely keen to have the broadest alliance possible.

The third person, who was perhaps most active as well as one of the strongest contenders for the top post, if not the strongest, was Mamata Banerjee of the Trinamool Congress (TMC) and the CM of Bengal. She was only second to Congress in terms of the number of MPs and her party was quite vocal about her credentials for the top role, even though she personally never stated the same. She continued to maintain the stance that the question for the PM candidature would arise only at an all-party meeting after the results were declared, where they will arrive at a consensus candidate. She had her strategy openly known when she laid bare her expectation that in the states where regional parties are strong, the national parties should support those parties, while national parties should fight in those states where they are in one to one fight with the BJP.

As per that formula, the Congress should support SP-BSP in UP and Aam Aadmi Party (AAP) in Delhi, while all the opposition parties should support congress in MP, Rajasthan, Chhattisgarh, Himachal Pradesh (HP) and all such states where Congress was in direct fight with BJP. This was also on the lines of what the Khan Market Gang had enumerated right in the very beginning – to have one opposition candidate per constituency against BJP/NDA. However, this strategy was extremely problematic, especially for the Congress, but also to Left parties. It would have meant that at all seats in West Bengal, it would be BJP vs TMC, which effectively left out Congress and Left from the electoral battle in West Bengal. Similarly, Congress would be out of Delhi too, in favour of AAP.

Hence, contradictions, conflicting interests, personal and party ambitions and, above all, big egos were all there in the open. The soft underbelly of the Mahagathbandhan was at full display. It needed a national party like the Congress to steer these conflicting priorities towards convergence. However, it appeared that Rahul – after his unexpected victory in MP, Rajasthan and Chhattisgarh – was blinded by hubris and expecting all others to approach him.

On 22 July 2018, it was reported that the Congress working committee had authorised Rahul Gandhi to forge a Grand National alliance for the 2019 Lok Sabha election to fight the BJP. When asked about the leadership, Congress-woman Ambika Soni said, "Naturally, he (Rahul) is the leader of the main national (opposition) party and we would want our leader to be the face of the opposition alliance." Rahul had himself openly expressed the desire to take on the PM role if Congress party won the maximum seats. Later on, perhaps for damage control, news appeared in the press that sources mentioned that Rahul personally would be keen to support a woman candidate for Prime Ministership. Other than these statements, there was no visible effort from the Congress on taking this mission forward.

And if there was at all an effort by Congress, it was woefully inadequate, as the nation was to realise on 12 January 2019, when Mayawati and Akhilesh announced their alliance for UP for the 2019 general elections, equally distributing 80 seats between the two of them, while unilaterally leaving out two seats of Amethi and Rae Bareilly for Rahul and Sonia, respectively. It was an open and royal snub to the Congress. One wonders why

Congress was treated with such disdain. It appeared as if both Akhilesh and Mayavati were irked with Congress. It looked like both of them were waiting for Rahul to approach them. After all, both of them had taken the initiative and come forward to provide unconditional support to Congress in Rajasthan and MP when they fell short of majority in the state elections in December 2018. In fact, in MP, Bahujan Samaj Party's (BSP) support was crucial in formation of Kamal Nath government. On the other hand, Rahul was sitting on his high horse, waiting for Mayawati and Akhilesh to pay him a visit. It appeared to be a perfect logjam.

Something similar happened with AAP. It was Arvind Kejriwal, who took the initiative and kept on pushing for an alliance across Delhi, Punjab and Haryana, but Congress kept on dithering. Eventually, after a long delay, when the back channel negotiations did start, cold water got poured over them when a twitter war, in full public view, erupted between Arvind and Rahul, blaming each other for being too difficult.

It was the same story in West Bengal and while Congress got the NCP alliance going, they missed an opportunity with a couple of smaller parties in Maharashtra. Rahul did get the Tamil Nadu alliance right, but that perhaps was the easiest of the lot. Despite parties like Dravida Munnetra Kazhagam (DMK) and Nationalist Congress Party (NCP) putting their weight behind Rahul, he felt way short of expectations, yet again.

If one was to go back to Rahul's press conference, post Congress victory in three states in December 2018, on his lessons on humility, the irony cannot be lost. Rahul perhaps should honestly reflect on the following questions:

Did he really internalise lessons on humility? Should he not have initiated alliance dialogues with opposition parties? Should he not have reached out, especially to Akhilesh and Mayawati, given that UP was most crucial to Mahagathbandan's fortunes, and given that, both had unilaterally come forward to help him in Rajasthan and MP?

While he accused Modi of not listening to the voice of the people, was he unable to hear that most opposition parties were not comfortable with his candidature for the PM's role and hence in that backdrop, should he really have publicly verbalised his ambition?

Bulleh Shah was right, ego is the real cause of most of man's problems! It makes you sit on your high horse while you go blind and deaf to even your well-wishers.

Victory can be a curse if not handled well. On the other hand, a defeat can be a boon if one draws the right lessons. If victory boosts your ego, it is a curse. If defeat makes you wiser, it is a boon. The momentum was with Congress, but apparently, their victories went to their head and clouded their wisdom. While BJP seemed to draw the right lessons from their defeats and acted wisely, victory pulled the Congress down and BJP rose from its defeat.

If you think of Rahul and Shah and you are given two words – arrogant and accommodative – asking to ascribe one of the words that best describes Rahul and the other to Shah. No one would blame you if you were to ascribe accommodative to Rahul and arrogant to Shah. However, if you take into consideration the whole alliance formation business, you will have to admit that swapping of words would be in order. Rahul was clearly arrogant and Shah evidently accommodative. As they say, appearances are deceptive. Maybe we should call it the power of illusions created by KMG and Lutyen's media.

In the end, it was a double whammy for the opposition. They could not form the Mahagathbandhan and yet the perception that had homed in with the public was that 2019 was a contest between Modi and the rest. BJP could not have asked for anything better and Modi leveraged this point to the hilt.

KMG's plans seem to have gone bust. Big egos appeared to have brought it down!

# 13
# It is the Welfare, Stupid!

## *July 2015, United Kingdom*

"India's share of the world economy when Britain arrived on its shores was 23%. By the time British left, it was down to below 4%. Why? Simply because India had been governed for the benefit of Britain. Britain's rise for two hundred years was financed by its depredations in India…"

These are the initial few lines of Shashi Tharoor, as he rose to speak at a debate at Oxford Union on whether Britain owed any reparations to its erstwhile colonies. Tharoor gave an impassioned, spirited and, goes without saying, an eloquent speech which was watched by scores of Indians, highly appreciated and even the Prime Minister lauded Tharoor for that. It is fair to say the Shashi at that moment touched a chord with all Indians who watched that speech and he deserved the standing ovation that he did get.

However, let's take the story forward from where Tharoor left, which is when British left and Congress took over, i.e. 1947 to 2014. What is astonishing is that the same lines which Tharoor narrated and produced above in the beginning of this chapter would still apply by just changing a few words. Let's see how:

"India's share of the world economy when Congress took over was below 4%. By the time UPA lost in 2014, it was down to below 3%. Why? Simply because India had been governed for the benefit of India's political dynasty. The dynasty's rise for seventy years was financed by its loot in India…."

If anyone was asked the question, who was most responsible for India's loot, the Mughal invaders, the British or Indian politicians, most people will give the same answer without batting an eyelid.

In July 2018, Modi made a startling revelation in Lok Sabha. He said when his government came to power in 2014, it noticed that public sector banks had been plundered. He remarked that in the sixty years since Independence, Indian banks had given loans worth eighteen lakh crore rupees, but from 2008 to 2014, in six years only, the loans had jumped to fifty-two lakh crores. A lot of these loans were given to cronies of the UPA government through phone banking, a euphemism he used for phone calls made to the banks by the powers that be at that time, allegedly pressurising them to grant loans to their cronies without any due diligence.

These loans would have been provided in the full knowledge that they would go bad and add to the bank's bad debts. Hence, interest rates would hardly matter, as irrespective of such rates, certain firms would be lent vast sums of money that would not be eventually recovered. Many unscrupulous businessmen seem to have exploited this system to accumulate personal wealth without caring to service debt. They would have known that the banks would have no option but to top it up with another loan and restructure it on more generous terms. This loan being repeated is what was later popularly known as evergreening of loans.

This way, the banks were alleged to have been looted during the UPA rule that laid the Non Productive Assets (NPA) landmine for Indian banks. Modi also mentioned that the banks fudged their records and showed only 2-2.5 lakh crores as NPA, whereas actually it was 9 lakh crores.

Legitimate taxpayer's hard-earned money appeared to be flowing out of the banks to unscrupulous players who used the money for illegitimate personal use that leads to running of a parallel black economy in the country. One of the indications of that is runaway inflation. Throughout the UPA2 years, the inflation averaged at 10% as prices soared. After all, the economy was flush with black money. There was too much money chasing few goods.

Around 2009-11, when the economy was really heating up and the inflation kept soaring, there were huge concerns expressed on black money in the country. In 2011, the finance ministry had asked a few independent agencies to estimate the amount of black money in the country.

Since then, reports were submitted to the finance ministry, but they have not been made public until today. However, *DNA* on 26 February 2019 reported through unnamed sources that one of the agencies – National Institute of Public Finance and Policy (NIPFP) – estimated that the unaccounted income during 2009-10 was as high as a whopping 72% of the GDP. Another agency – National Council of Applied Economic Research (NCAER) – estimated the black money to be in the range of 71-79% of the GDP during 2009-11.

A well-known economist, Arun Kumar, former professor of JNU, had estimated black economy to be 62.02% of the GDP in 2012 in his article that was published in *Economic and Political*

*Weekly* in its 26 November 2016 edition. There have been many such studies conducted by known experts and institutions over the years and the range varies from anywhere between 40 to 75%. The other worrying aspect to note is that all such studies during that period clearly showed an increasing trend. Arun Kumar estimated that black money had grown by around 20% in the five years leading up to 2012.

The anecdotal experience also bore this out. If we recall, during those days, people had no option but to pay out cash anywhere between 50-60% of the total cost when they went to buy a property or a flat. Similarly, most of the purchases of private vehicles also used to be on cash. According to a 2015 report by PricewaterhouseCoopers (PWC), a renowned audit firm, at that time 98% of all transactions by volume used to happen in cash, and 68% of the total value of transactions were in cash.

There is a view among a few economists, and certainly, the UPA regimes seem to ascribe to the view that black money helps economic growth. Example of the real estate sector is given, which is one of the major generators of black money that keeps the sector primed, hence leading to its growth that in turn provides jobs to so many poor. That argument is lopsided, but before we crush it, we need to consider another hard reality.

In 1985, on a visit to drought-affected Kalahandi district in Odisha, the then Prime Minister Rajiv Gandhi had famously said that of every one rupee spent by the government on poor, only fifteen paisa reached the intended beneficiary. Who would know better than the Prime Minister! So now, we come back to the black money helping the economy argument. If only fifteem paisa of the legitimate one rupee allocated by a legitimate government reached the poor, how much of a rupee of black money passing through informal channels, actually reach the poor? Much less, one would reasonably assume.

Hence, people who argue in favour of black money as a booster of growth, miss on the basics of human nature. In a jungle economy, which is what black economy is, the might is always right. The influential and the most powerful of the people will pocket most of the black money, allowing just a trickle to go down. It leads to scams, rapacious greed, vulgar display of wealth and hoarding. To top it, the worst of the human behaviour is at display in the dark economy. The income disparities grow, the rich become richer and the poor are left reeling with all the adverse fallouts of the black 'parallel' economy, like inflation, etc.

Going back to the real estate example, the sector grew, property prices appreciated, rich people made huge profits, but since most of it was black, the government was not paid by commensurate taxes that would have been utilised to fund welfare schemes for the poor. Eventually the sector went bust!

Black economy booster can just be a temporary steroid and as they say, finally, karma always catches up. All this black money was to eventually suck the banks dry. Scams started tumbling out of the closets, put breaks on credit, leading to economic activity slowing down eventually. This is exactly what happened, if one recollects the last days of the UPA regime.

Growth in the last quarters had fallen to 4.5%, there was runaway inflation leading to prices skyrocketing, people were being forced to convert their hard-earned money into black for major purchases like housing, capitation to schools/colleges, etc., scams were a dime a dozen all over the place, leading to a complete policy paralysis.

It was an extremely despondent atmosphere when the people saw hope and put their faith in Narendra Modi in 2014. This was also one of the main reasons why people supported Modi on demonetisation, as they saw it as a genuine and sincere effort to get the country out of the morass of black money. The parallel economy was taking over the system and had run its limits as far as the patience of people was concerned. Hence, they willingly backed Modi's genuine and sincere attempt to clean up the system.

The other key financial reform was the Goods and Services Tax (GST), which decisively moved the country towards one nation one tax doctrine. This was in the works for over a decade but again it took the decisive leadership of Modi and deft handling by Arun Jaitley, the then finance minister, to make it see the light of the day. The overall businesses registered under GST went up to one crore from an earlier figure of sixty-four lakhs. The cumulative effect of demonetisation as well as GST was that as per CRISIL (a global analytical company providing ratings, research, risk and policy advisory services), the income tax increased from 8.2% in financial year (FY) 2016 to 26.8% in financial year 2017, and 21% in financial year 2018. The income tax filings nearly doubled in the five years of Modi regime.

We cannot lose sight of some of the other critical policy measures that Modi undertook before demonetisation. In 2015, Reserve Bank of India (RBI) regulations for banks were tightened to ensure identification of NPAs promptly, recovery of loans, liquidations and sale of companies that defaulted on loans in a time-bound manner. These laws and rules were important to clean up the mess in banking and check the flow of black money into the market. Benami Act was given teeth to punish owners who hedged money in benami properties. The government negotiated tax treaties with tax havens like Switzerland, Mauritius, Singapore, Panama, etc., to check money laundering and ensuring transparency in banking transactions of Indians in foreign banks by agreeing to share data on real time basis.

Banks, businesses, properties and foreign money transactions were the key focus areas of the Modi government to check black money. These and many other measures taken during the Modi government's first tenure had helped to bring back Rs 1.3 lakh crores as per official government records. Until last count, the banks had been already able to recover Rs 4 lakh crore of loans from the defaulting companies.

Modi was closing the tap which allowed the free flow of money out into the black economy and applying a suction pump to start sucking back the black money stuck in the quagmire of corruption. As Modi would famously claim at many of his public meetings from time to time, "During UPA regime, we used to hear how much money was leaving the government coffers through money laundering and corruption, and now people are hearing how much is coming back."

On the other side, Modi started a massive drive of financial inclusion of the poor by having their bank accounts opened up for free, under Jan Dhan Yojana. The opposition mocked this drive, calling it a meaningless exercise and asked the rationale for the scheme when, as per them, the accounts would only remain empty. In five years, Modi government had opened up more than thirty-six crore accounts and almost all the poor had been covered. Next, Modi linked up these accounts with the Aadhaar number as well as their mobile numbers with the key purpose of ensuring Direct Benefit Transfer (DBT) of monies paid to these poor as subsidies, into their respective Jan Dhan accounts.

Since 2014-15, the government had transferred 7.23 lakh crore of subsidies directly into the bank accounts of the poor. Through the DBT, government plugged subsidy leakages by eliminating intermediaries, middlemen and fictitious accounts of undeserving people. In this way, they were able to save over 1.4 lakh crore. Circa 2019, the one rupee that was allocated for the poor, the whole of that rupee was going directly to their respective bank accounts. As Modi was closing on the tap on black money, in parallel, he had opened up another tap, with no leakages, through which poured out welfare schemes for the poor.

To establish a welfare state is the fundamental objective of modern-day democratic governments and especially if it is a developing country like India, still in the process of eradicating poverty. There are two critical terms economists use in welfare economics – first is 'value judgements', which, in a layman's language means that if you have limited resources, which is mostly true for a government in a developing country like India, then you ought to choose a scheme or a policy that makes the maximum number of people better off and the least number of people worse off. As the state makes these value judgments, it must base it on ethics which is the second critical term. Needless to say, 'ethics' become even more critical for a resource-scarce country like India, where so many compete for limited resources. An ethical response makes it incumbent on the government of the day, that maximum government resources are allocated to and reach the most deserving of the people.

If we judge the UPA as well as the NDA regime on these two parameters, the difference is obvious. UPA seemed to believe in giving a booster to the economy at the top, encouraging unethical behaviour, expecting development to automatically trickle down to the poor. The schemes meant for the disadvantaged suffered heavy leakages and only a measly bit seemed to reach the most deserving.

On the other hand, Modi decoupled economy and development, in the sense that he made economy a means to an end rather than the end in itself with regards to development. He started cleaning the economy while it was still doing well, which is exactly when it should be done; closed the black money tap and opened up a leakage-proof development tap for the poor. The 'unethical' tap, which primarily served the already rich and mighty, allowing only a trickle to reach the poor, was shut and an 'ethical' tap opened up which gushed out welfare schemes unencumbered directly to the poor. It was a paradigm shift in Indian welfare economics.

Indian government has always had a hand in big business, popularly termed as Crony socialism. Nehru started it with the 'license quota raj' and since then it was widely known that businesses close to the government would get undue advantages from the government. In the UPA regimes, it had been taken to another level with corruption scandals in the allocation of resources, i.e. 2G, Coal, etc. And then we had what Modi called the phone banking culture of disbursing loans, without any accountability, to businesses deemed close to the government. Modi had put a stop to all that by bringing in laws to make businesses accountable for repaying back the loans, and by introducing banking policies to make banks accountable for disbursing loans while ensuring that the government had no hand in big business. He had struck at the heart of the Nehruvian order.

# 14
# The Final Salvos

A few months before the 2019 elections, Modi fired his first of the last few salvos from his well-equipped war chest. In September 2018, he announced the Ayushman Bharat medical insurance scheme for the ten crore poor families, covering over fifty crore people across India. It was deemed as the biggest health care scheme of the world as it covered a total number of people equivalent to the populations of USA, Canada and Mexico put together.

As he had provided a single-minded focus on the implementation of the welfare schemes throughout his first term, he wanted to ensure that on the last leg, his governance engine was totally fired up and his salvos started getting some real quick hits. In the first month itself, one lakh beneficiaries had availed of the healthcare benefits, and by April 2019, the numbers had crossed twenty lakhs. Three crores families had already been issued cards by April. The engine was moving at a frenetic pace.

While unconfirmed reports had started doing the rounds much earlier that Congress party was looking to announce a bumper universal basic income scheme as a poll promise to trump Modi, it was only in late January 2019 that Rahul finally announced at a rally, Congress's commitment to a Minimum Income Guarantee for the poor to eradicate poverty. At that time, no amount was disclosed, neither were any further details given. Actually, the then chief economic advisor, Arvind Subramanian to the Modi government, first mooted the idea in 2017. He had proposed a cash payout as a minimum income to the poor households instead of all the subsidies that were being given. Reports suggested that he had recommended a sum of eighteen thousand rupees per annum to take care of the minimum subsistence level of poverty.

This was being considered as a huge game changer. Post the victory of Congress in the three states of MP, Chhattisgarh and Rajasthan, the mood within the party had changed for the better and this scheme would just tilt the scales in their favour decisively, the Congress would have thought. Hectic conjectures on the basic income started doing the rounds on media, and more importantly, people were keen to know how Modi would counter this game changer, if at all. All eyes were on Modi's interim budget now.

On 1 February 2019, Piyush Goyal, then officiating as Finance Minister in place of Arun Jaitley who was indisposed, presented the final interim budget of the Modi government. Sure enough, all the final salvos in Modi's war chest were launched at this budget. Piyush announced a big tax relief for the middle class, giving full rebate to all taxable incomes below five lakhs. He also announced 10% reservation for the economically weaker sections of the general category students in higher education institutions. The final salvo, the *brahmastra*, Pradhan Mantri Kisan Samman Nidhi, popularly called PM-Kisan was also launched.

This scheme was for 12 crore farmers across the country who owned and cultivated 5 acres and less. The government would pay 2000 rupees per instalment, three times a year, to supplement the financial needs of the small and marginal farmers for procuring seeds and other inputs to ensure crop health and improvement in yields. This scheme was going to cost the government over 75,000 crore rupees. More importantly, Modi promised to pay out the first instalment to farmers before 1 March 2019. Sure enough, the first payout was made by Modi on 24 February 2019 at Gorakhpur, and the first instalment was paid to over one crore farmers.

Rahul had expressed his intention of launching a Universal Basic Income scheme in January 2019 but Modi went ahead and not just announced his variant of income scheme but also implemented the same by end of February while Rahul was yet to announce his own. Modi always stressed on his Kaamdaar (a doer) image through his focus on implementation of schemes, not just announcing them. At these last critical moments, he wanted to leave no stone unturned to further reinforce this image and project a stark contrast with Rahul, whom he called the Naamdaar (survives on name).

At rallies, he would take a dig at Congress for just announcing schemes and doing little further than that. He would very often remind people of Congress's *garibi hatao* (remove poverty) slogan, which Indira Gandhi gave in 1971, but she and her successive governments did very little about implementing it.

Finally, on 25 March 2019, Rahul announced his own surgical strike on poverty called Nyuntam Aay Yojana (NYAY). He promised to pay bottom of the 20% of the poor families six thousand rupees per month. This was a scheme worth 3.6 lakh crores and would cover 25 crore individuals across the country. Rahul looked extremely cheerful and pumped up at the press conference he held for this launch. One got an impression that he was thinking he already had the election 2019 in his bag. He perhaps was guilty of counting the chickens before they hatched.

"A bird in hand is worth two in the bush," Modi seemed to understand the importance of this adage very well. While Rahul was taking time to announce Congress's NYAY, Modi had already gone ahead, announced and made sure that the first instalment of PM-Kisan reached the farmers.

# 15
# When the Monkey Flew

***Around 5000 BC, somewhere on the southernmost tip of Ancient India:***

Hanuman to Jaamvant: Kapishreshtha (tallest among monkeys), allow me to go. You know my powers, it will just take me one leap and I will be at Lanka. I can reach mata Sita within no time.

Jaamvant: No, Vaayuputra (son of the Wind god), I cannot allow you to go. It is too risky. Your leap could well trigger a war and put all of us all in trouble.

Hanuman: Please, I can finish this myself.

Jaamvant: No, I cannot allow you to do this, sorry.

...and the monkey-god never flew!

The above is a famous episode in Ramayana at the time when Lord Ram finally came to know that Ravan had kidnapped Sita and taken her to Lanka, his capital. Everyone was trying to figure out how to reach Lanka. It actually did not quite happen the way mentioned above. Jaamvant actually reminded Hanuman of his powers and motivated him to take the leap, but imagine if it had actually happened the way potrayed above. Actually, something similar happened in Delhi after the 26/11/2008 Mumbai attacks.

As New Delhi was mulling over the response to Pakistan, our Vaayu Sena (Air Force) promptly offered to give Pakistan a befitting response. The request was swiftly rejected by the government of the day, and instead it chose to give a meek diplomatic response.

## *26 February 2019. Hoshiarpur, Punjab*

Hoshiarpur is a small, sleepy city in Punjab. People go about doing their chores at quite a leisurely pace, mostly satisfied and content with the way things are, though a lament or two with the general administration or politics is always in order. The youngsters are a bit more impatient, ambitious and see their true salvation in Canada. That is pretty much the standard short story of any small town or city in India, except of course the choice of place of salvation may vary depending on the state one hails from. Hence, for Punjab, if it is Canada, for someone from UP or Bihar, it might be Delhi. For Kolkata, Kerala, maybe Middle East… so on and so forth.

It was between 2:30 a.m. and 3:00 a.m. An old lady, who due to her medication, had to frequent the toilet very often at night, had woken up for one such trip. She heard the scorching sound of a jet fighter, cut through the silence of the night. One led to another and then there were many strands of sound indicating that there were several jets flying together. Being close to the Pakistan border and having an Air Force base close by, she was used to the jets flying around, but at this unearthly hour and so many of them! She thought this was rather unusual. Nonetheless, after giving it some more thought and completing her own sortie, she slid back into the cosy confines of her quilt.

Next morning, she got the real import of what she had experienced the previous night. Unwittingly, she had witnessed history in the making. For an ordinary person hailing from a place that is in the middle of nowhere, that perhaps was the closest shave that one could have with history. "Operation Bandar" had been executed successfully. India Air Force had struck a terrorist camp, Balakot, right in the heart of Pakistan, just sixty kilometres away from Abbottabad where Osama was hiding before the American forces killed him. Scores of terrorists and their masters were killed. Indian jets had crossed the international border and India crossed the Rubicon that day. The name 'Operation Bandar' was perhaps a tribute to the monkey king, Lord Hanuman.

The disappointment of having been denied the chance to serve the country in 2008 had now been overcome. It was not just to showcase a hollow bravado that the Indian Air Force had raised its hand back then. They knew they had the capability to give a proportionate response and hit the enemy where it hurt the most. Perhaps, back then, it was an opportunity lost. India could have easily gone on a jugular and since the whole world had witnessed the horrific incident, it would have understood India's right to respond. However, the go-ahead never came. This time it was different, though. The Vayu Sena was given a free hand and the monkey finally flew. Lord Hanuman would have smiled!

14 February 2019 was a fateful day when a Jaish-e-Mohammad (JeM) suicide bomber killed forty Central Reserve Police Force (CRPF) jawans at Pulwama in Jammu & Kashmir. Immediately after that, Modi had sworn revenge at a time and place of his choosing. However, it was a very sensitive time. General elections were less than two months away and political parties were already in campaigning mode. All opinion surveys

were suggesting that NDA was ahead of UPA. That was when Modi had not even started campaigning full steam. His ability to electrify the atmosphere is legendary and he would have been sure to pull over many more voters to his side as the elections came closer. Nobody would have faulted him if he had chosen to remain quiet through the election period.

It was too risky a call to go ahead with concrete action before elections. If at all he did, the action clearly had to be much more spectacular than the surgical strikes, and during that action, in case there was collateral damage, Modi could have easily lost the election. We saw when Wing Commander Abhinandan was caught by the Pakistanis, how the mood throughout the country had gone suddenly sullen. Candle light marches had begun and the weak hearts, of which there is no dearth in India, were on the streets. Had Abhinandan not been released for a few more days, the mood would have changed from sullenness to anger, and who knows where it would have stopped. Imagine if we had lost a few soldiers. It would have been a disaster.

However, Modi being Modi, had the penchant to take tough calls, given his personality trait that we discussed early on in the book. The predominance of rational ability enables him to possess absolute clarity on what the purpose, goals and intended outcomes are. India had made it clear with surgical strikes that henceforth, no misadventure would go unpunished. Once Pulwama happened, it was clear that the response had to be proportionate and even more spectacular than the surgical strikes. The forces were given a free hand. Razor sharp intelligence agencies were able to trace a great opportunity and the Air Force executed it to near perfection. Not a single loss of precious life of our armed forces or even innocents on the other side of the border and the whole nation went through a collective surge of nationalistic fervour that could have very easily been a pall of gloom.

It was the first time after 1971 that Indian Air Force had crossed the international border with Pakistan. India had called Pakistan's nuclear bluff and pushed the nuclear threshold. More importantly, by reinforcing a muscular policy, Modi had very clearly distinguished himself from the soft approach of the earlier UPA regime. India, for long, was perceived as a soft nation. Nehru's Matang muni had finally been given a permanent burial. Critics had panned surgical strikes as one-off and not really a part of a carefully thought-out doctrine. In hindsight, perhaps Balakot strikes would prove to be that watershed event when India shed off its soft nation tag permanently. Unfortunately, the world does not pay heed to your messages of love, compassion and peace unless you are strong and powerful.

In a well-known poem, Ramdhari Singh Dinkar once wrote:

*Sehensheelta, kshamaa, dayaa ko*
*Tabhi poojta jug hai*
*Bal ka darp chamakta uske*
*Peechhe jabb jagmag hai.*
*(The world bows to your tolerance, forgiveness and kindness, only when your immense strength shines through brightly from behind you, for all to see.)*

It is the difficult moments such as the Pulwana attack that really test one's convictions in one's beliefs, which one publicly espouses. It is moments such as these where the public watches quietly, whether you practice what you preach and live up to it. In the most trying of circumstances, Modi lived up to it!

# Part III

# *Battle to Win 'Trust'*

# 16
# Hamara Neta Kaisa Ho...

On 10 March 2019, the Election Commission of India announced that the 2019 general election would be held in seven phases from 11 April – 19 May 2019 to constitute the seventeenth Lok Sabha. The votes would be counted and results declared on 23 May 2019. The poll bugle had been blown; the battle to win the trust of people had begun.

How should our leader be? Most political analysts wrestle with this question. It is such a broad subject that different folks will pinpoint different aspects. However, there seems to be a near unanimity among most political experts that the most important element in winning elections is 'trust'. Then comes the million-dollar question, how does a leader or a political party win people's trust. What attributes or characteristics go into building trust with voters or citizens. In leadership and management studies, many researches have been done on the subject of trust in the past, across many organisations, which can be applied to political organisations too, as it is all about winning over, managing, motivating and influencing people.

The book – taking advantage of the author's over two-and-a-half decades of rich and vast experience in the fields of leadership, behavioural sciences as well as his deep understanding of politics – has developed a trust model. It would help outline the key factors for leaders and political parties that play a major role in building trust with the citizens. These all-encompassing factors cover all the key traits like sincerity, enthusiasm, competence, etc., as well as several others, and provides the key parameters on which even the citizens can easily evaluate various leaders and political parties to make an informed decision on whom they should choose.

There are four key factors, encapsulating all critical attributes essential for building trust, and they are as follows:

- Clarity of higher purpose
- Credibility (deliver on promises)
- Connect with people
- Lead by example

In the following chapters, the book considers each of these four factors in detail, in the backdrop of how politics played out ever since Modi took over as Prime Minister in May 2014, right up to the last vote cast in May 2019. In the process, it covers all the key highlights of Modi's election campaign as well as that of Rahul Gandhi and evaluates them on the four factors for building trust outlined above.

Both of them, put together, conducted more than two hundred and fifty rallies across India during the election campaign, post the Election Commission's formal declaration of elections and the election dates. Hence, as people analysed these two individuals and parties as they went around the country for over two months, so does the book evaluate them on the trust model as it tracked their election campaign.

# 17
# Clarity of Higher Purpose

Why do a party and its leadership exist? This goes to the heart of a party's ideology that guides the leader to articulate his purpose in a way that it connects with the people. Of course, to resonate with the citizens spontaneously, it has to be relevant to the context in which it operates. Hence, there are two critical aspects to this factor – First, a party has to have a higher purpose, and second, it has to fulfil the needs of the people.

World peace is a great purpose, but will it connect with the vast majority of people who are reeling in poverty and finding it difficult to make ends meet. The answer is a big 'NO'. As someone has said, "Content is king but context is kingdom". Purpose has to fit the context in which it is applied. World peace is a great goal for United Nations, not for a political party in India.

Purpose is the pole star; it acts as a guiding light to the party and its leaders, especially when it is facing dilemmas, decisive moments and challenging situations. As we argued in a chapter earlier, how tough decision like Balakot strikes could not have been made unless there was total clarity of the purpose. Very importantly, it also acts as a moral compass, and keeps reminding its followers the importance of ethics and values, a rare commodity in today's politics.

Demonetisation was such a risky call for Modi. He put his political survival at stake, but he was more concerned about doing the ethical thing. Guided by the purpose of his party, he was keen to bring ethics back in the economy and clean it up. Above all, the higher purpose is about altruism; it is the fundamental reason why parties exist – to care, serve and help people.

To understand this tenet better, it is worthwhile to consider the example of India National Congress (INC) from pre-Independence days. When Bapu arrived in India from South Africa in 1915, the INC, which was founded in 1885, was divided between the Moderates and the Extremists. The Moderates wanted more Indian participation in the government under British rule itself, while the Extremists wanted complete independence. Bal Gangadhar Tilak was leading the Extremists and Gopal Krishna Gokhale was the voice of the Moderates. Thus, there was no unity of purpose amongst the Congressmen, which was a divided house. On the other hand, whatever the objective or objectives of the Congress, they did not really resonate with the masses. Simply because these goals were far removed from the immediate survival needs of the poverty-stricken people of India. Hence, Congress neither had a cogent purpose that all Congressmen agreed to or had unanimity on, and neither did it connect with a large section of the people.

In such a situation, Congress was mainly restricted to a following among a few educated, well-to-do people, while most Indians, living in abject poverty and reeling under the burden of a plethora of social evils, really had no connect with it. It was Bapu, who took it as his life's purpose to improve the day-today lives of poor Indians, their livelihood, education, sanitation, and rid them of social evils like untouchability. Congress eventually united behind the way shown by Bapu, and it was this sense of purpose, and not the goal for India's freedom struggle, that resonated the most with the millions of Indians, who subsequently followed Bapu to change the course of India's independence movement. A party can make revolutions happen, if they have a higher goal clearly defined, agreed and aligned to the needs of the masses.

Cut to 2014, Manmohan Singh's UPA government was reeling under serious corruption charges, policy paralysis had become a popular lexicon and economy was going through its worst slow-down in years, inflation was in double digits and prices were sharply rising, affecting the poor in the most adverse way. Add to that a constant threat of terrorism that had led to serial bomb blasts killing hundreds of innocent people and had become a major security concern among the people. In this backdrop arrived Modi. As they say, cometh the hour, cometh the man, driven by his party's ideology to making India stronger by uplifting its people, starting with weakest person of the society (*antyodaya*). *Antyodaya*, as was discussed in an earlier chapter, is the key purpose, along with making India strong, that drives the BJP.

Modi articulated a positive agenda of development, good governance and a promise to give a strong response to terrorism and eventually to root it out, that resonated immensely with the people. It was for the first time in Indian politics that development was the main plank for an Indian election. What Modi promised was in alignment to the core purpose of BJP and the need of the hour for the people. Hence, in 2014, BJP polled

66% more votes than 2009 and Congress lost 33%, resulting in Modi becoming the Prime Minister.

Year 2019 was going to be more challenging for Modi than 2014, when he was himself the challenger. However, guided by his party ideology, he embarked on the right path very early on in his first innings. He stressed on welfare schemes for the poor and marginalised, from the front. He focused on building houses, providing gas cylinders, electricity and building rural roads to improve connectivity. He resolved for financial inclusion of the poor by opening up their bank accounts. These bank accounts were soon to become key vessels through which subsidies for various welfare schemes would directly flow to the poor, stopping the leakages, and removing the scourge of corruption from the day-to-day lives of the poor. Without wasting much time, he had promptly put antyodayain action and that remained Modi's key focus area, right through his term.

In that sense, 2019 was a continuation and reinforcement of the same resolve. A lot had happened, but a lot more needed to happen. There were still many who were yet to taste the fruit of development and hence the expectations from Modi had gone a notch higher. Sensing the mood, Modi made an even stronger pitch for development in 2019, making a renewed commitment to take development to a new level.

"In the last five years, we were busy taking care of basic needs. In the next five years, we will work on fulfilling the aspirations of people," he said. He promised to hasten the pace of development works and committed to providing housing for all by 2022. He talked about harnessing the youth power of India and encouraged them to look at becoming employers rather than being employed. He went on to talk about the Mudra scheme. He reiterated the government's resolve to doubling farmer income and added one more to his already long list of commitments – of providing piped drinking water to all by 2024. '*Nal mein jal*' as their election manifesto said.

This ability to understand the real needs of the people and aligning them with the higher purpose of the party is a key factor for the success of a political party. Modi and BJP, in the current scenario, seem to understand the pulse of the nation well. In fact, BJP called its election manifesto 'Sankalp Patra' (commitment manifesto) to mark their honest intent and demonstrate their determination to fulfil all the promises made in it. While making all these promises, they would cut across caste, creed and religion and never miss to make the point that development is for all and not selective – *Sabka saath, sabka vikas*.

His achievements on national security were marked by theatrics and display of an array of emotions during most of the more than hundred rallies he conducted in his election campaign, which got a huge approval from the masses. His '*ghar me ghus ke marenge*' (will enter the house and hit) comment created a frenzy among people at one of his rallies and the whole arena reverberated with the chant of 'Modi, Modi'.

Modi gets dollops of energy and enthusiasm from the core purpose of the party. This dialogue was played out on national TV repeatedly, marking India's permanent shift to a more muscular policy towards Pakistan and strengthening national security. Comments like, "*Kisi ko chhedna nahi he, lekin kisi ne chheda to chhodna nahi hai*" (we won't trouble anyone, but if someone troubles us, then we won't spare them) were instant hits and would draw rapturous applause. The point he was driving home was that there were going to be consequences for any misadventure by India's adversaries and that they would be so harsh and spectacular that the enemy will think twice before striking next.

As discussed earlier in the book, the Communist party has had a motivated and committed cadre, but their base has been shrinking rapidly. Well, the first broader point is that their higher purpose does not resonate with the people of the country. Actually, it is not just in India but world over that their ideology is crumbing. Russia, communism's biggest mascot, broke into pieces. China is thriving only because it has adopted Capitalism. They will have to either reinvent their purpose or wait for the time when their narrative starts to echo with the people.

Second, and perhaps the more fundamental point is that the party itself seems to have digressed from their stated purpose. Their hatred for Modi has made them blind to their own purpose. All people see and hear are their constant and continuous rants against Modi and their blind opposition to every policy of the government, merely to oppose Modi. Why? Because as they put it, he is fascist and anti-secular.

Firstly, they should try to teach a lesson on secularism to a distressed farmer or a person who is struggling to feed his family two square meals a day. Secondly, their mindless diatribe against Modi, without any proof, when he has such a positive image in the minds of the people, is like digging their own grave. Communism in India has degenerated to anti-Modi-ism. It seems they have forgotten their own agenda. Rather than promoting their own philosophy, proposed policies and direction, they have reduced themselves to becoming a spare tyre for any anti-Modi vehicle. Their sole agenda is to get rid of Modi by any means. For that, they are even ready to tie up with the most corrupt.

These 'azadi' and 'tukre tukre' slogans by their associates may well be germinating the seeds of 'azadi' from and 'tukre tukre' of the communist parties, in the minds of the silent aspirational Indians.

Additionally, most of what has been said about the communists above is true for Congress too. However, there is a lot else that needs to be talked about the party and it begins with asking the existential question – what is it that Congress exists for? What is it that drives Congress?

Congressmen will themselves tell you – "The family". They openly state that. In fact, it seems like a matter of pride that if the family is not there, the Congress will cease to exist. This usually happens when a party or an organisation has lost its ideological moorings. This is when they take refuge in a person or a set of people, rather than seeking an anchor in the ideology. Political pundits generally agree that the only thing that keeps Congress going is power, and their belief is that Gandhis are their best bet to attain power. To get to power, they needed to remove Modi. Hence, it is no surprise that most of election campaign of the Congress – indeed of the whole of opposition – revolved around discrediting Modi. That appeared to have become their real purpose.

Hence the term *'Chowkidar chor hai'*. Modi was the villain of the piece. Rahul did over a hundred rallies and he had a standard script that ran as follows:

"Modi's government was the government of 15-20 richest people of India and all happened to be industrialists. Modi was, in fact, the *chowkidar* (security person) of the rich as he allowed them loan waiver to the tune of 5.55 lakh crores. Through demonetisation, Modi snatched money from the hands of the poor and gave it to these 15 industrialists. In the Rafale deal, the then French President told him that the French were directed to give the contract to Anil Ambani and he got a bonanza of Rs. 45,000 crores. The list of 15 richest people included folks like Vijay Mallya, Nirav Modi, Mehul Chowksi, Lalit Modi, who were allowed by Modi to run away."

Then came the list of all the lies Modi told the people of India. First, he would pick on the alleged fifteen lakh rupees in every account promise made by Modi. With a lot of rage, he would go on to say that while Modi never delivered on the 15 lakh, he promises to pay 3.6 lakh crore rupees per year to the 20% poorest people of India and would go on to roll out his proposed NYAY scheme. On the issue of where the money would come from, he had a very simple and straightforward reply. The money was going to come from Anil Ambani's pocket – all the money that Modi had freely distributed to these fifteen richest people, all that money that belonged to the poor, Rahul was going to take all that money out from their pockets and give it back to the poor.

The next lie about Modi was on the jobs front. He claimed that Modi had promised two crore jobs per year to the youth, but that never happened. He mentioned how the unemployment level had been the highest in the last fory-five years under Modi, and he had promised to fill up 22 lakh vacant government jobs by March 2020, create 10 lakh jobs at the panchayat level and completely liberalise setting up of new businesses that would require no permission or paper work for the first three years.

Finally, he would lay a frontal attack on Modi's atrocities on the farmers and tribals. He alleged that Modi was putting all the farmers behind bars, for non-repayment of loans. As an extension, he promised that the Congress would actually waive off all loans. He would then go on to remind the tribals how the UPA had brought in the bill to protect their rights while Modi was directing the authorities to shoot tribals.

There was no reference to development, national security and governance matters – subjects that even the opinion surveys found top-most in the minds of the voters. The key takeaway from Rahul's speeches was that Modi was responsible for all ills (imaginary or otherwise) in India, and hence, he must be removed at any cost.

In terms of a future vision, there was a promise of a dole package, which was to be incredulously funded by the richest of the country. The response to his pronouncement was, at best, lukewarm. An aspirational India seemed to have moved on from such promises and perhaps was no longer enamoured by the promise of charity. Congress looked completely out of touch. It showed Rahul's, but more importantly Congress's, bankruptcy when it comes to ideology and purpose. Hate Modi or perpetuate a particular dynasty cannot be an ideology or purpose. It has to be something more sublime and positive.

On the other hand, Modi – even though he was critical of his opponents – continued to stress on a much more positive agenda. More importantly, these themes vibrated well with the people. Take the example of the promise of providing drinking water. It is a huge issue across India, especially in drought-stricken as well as rural India. No other party had thought of making it a poll issue, but Modi did. A party and a leader committed to a higher ideal would always have their eyes and ears to the ground. BJP had a higher purpose, and more importantly, Modi never let it go out of sight and was constantly guided by it.

The other advantage of a clearly-stated core purpose that connects with people is that the exalted cause draws the appropriate type of people towards the party and its leaders. You can be certain that Modi was drawn to the cause of antyodaya and selfless service to the nation when he joined the BJP. He selflessly served the party and only took on administrative responsibility because he was required by the top leadership to go and manage the crisis with the BJP in Gujarat. He was well over fifty years of age at that time. Modi's critics say that he is highly ambitious and can do anything to remain in power. Well, facts do not bear that out.

Someone who assumes a position of power only after fifty years of age, that too on being directed to take charge rather than on his own volition, cannot be labelled as ambitious. Until that time, he had never even fought a school election. Someone who did not even have a bank account until then and lived a Spartan life, always remaining in the background while happily serving the party – you do not call that person ambitious. Yes, he may be ambitious for the country and its people, but definitely not for his own self.

Modi is not the only one; there are scores of people like him in BJP. Modi himself would have drawn motivation from people like Vajpayee and Advani, who were themselves working selflessly, building the party and inspiring the cadre in earlier times. The salutary effect of the core purpose on BJP cadres has been discussed in an earlier chapter. However, it will be apt to highlight a couple of examples here. Sunil Deodhar, BJP National Secretary, was one of the key persons to have turned around Tripura state for the BJP. He was also the key person on the ground in West Bengal, who helped BJP win 18 seats in Bengal in Lok Sabha elections. Both these victories were nothing short of spectacular. In fact, unprecedented.

Another example is of Sunil Bansal, State General Sectratary of BJP for UP. He was the main man on the ground in UP for Amit Shah, both during the state elections in 2017, and Lok Sabha elections in 2014 as well as 2019. He is one of the key reasons for BJP's spectacular performance in UP. Both these men have such stupendous achievements to their credit, and yet, we do not hear much about them. They, and many others like them, are the unsung real heroes behind BJP's success. They are happy to serve the party and remain in the background without seeking any administrative office or privileges for themselves, driven only by the higher purpose and ideals of the party.

If the party's purpose, as understood by people, is sublime, it will draw more people with higher ideals. And if the purpose is selfish and petty, it will attract more rent seekers.

# 18
# Credibility (Deliver on Promises)

If one was required to pick up the most important attribute to build trust, credibility will be the one. Creating a right sense of purpose, fixing goals, but not delivering on it, will erode the trust of people. Hence, you not only have to say what you will do, but do what you say! In addition to sincerity, commitment and your ability to shoulder responsibility tests one's competence and capability.

Bapu's reputation preceded him when he returned to India in 1915. He had successfully employed *satyagraha* (non-violent resistance) for civil rights in South Africa. He politically mobilised the Indian-origin South Africans and helped found Natal Indian Congress. Hence, on his return to India, people had high expectations from him. He did not belie those expectations and successfully led his first satyagraha movement for Indigo farmers in Champaran, Bihar and subsequently for Ahmedabad mill workers. He forced the imperial power to come down and mutually agree on a peaceful settlement with the farmers and labourers. Indians had tasted their first victories against the British Raj. Gandhi had delivered and had become a 'Mahatma'.

In 2014, Modi came with the reputation of a *vikas purush* (man of development), having been a successful chief minister for three consecutive terms. His Gujarat model of development was hailed as the model to be emulated not just by the other states, but the centre too. He was viewed as a man of action who was decisive and non-corruptible. Modi's strong reputation eventually catapulted him to the Prime Minister's role back then.

In 2019, he lived up to the image that he had come with and had a strong performance to showcase. The report card looked excellent. Around 10 crore toilets were built, sanitation coverage had increased from 39% in 2014 to over 95% in 2019. More than 7 crore free gas connections; 1.5 crore *pucca* (concrete) houses built (as against 25 lakhs in UPA2); highway and rail network built at over twice the speed than under the UPA2; Ayushman Bharat medical healthcare scheme covering 10 crore poor families; PM-Kisan covering 12 crore farmers who had under 5 acres of land and many others such schemes for the under priviledged. Amit Shah, as he unveiled a new BJP slogan – *Saaf Niyat, Sahi Vikas* – mentioned that the Modi government had benefitted 22 crore poor families with its welfare schemes.

On what Amit Shah said, even if half these numbers were true, that still would have been a phenomenal performance. No government in the past has had such a deep and penetrative impact on the lives of the poor. Talking about toilets, rural women would show their appreciation by saying that Modi has given them an essential, their *izzat ghar*. On gas connections, they would say that only a son of a poor mother could have thought of that.

The other thing Modi stressed on was governance. There was not even a hint of a corruption charge – notwithstanding the smoke-screen of Rafale – against him or his government. Direct benefit transfer of more than 7.5 lakh crores in over 430 government schemes through JAM (Jan Dhan bank accounts, Aadhaar, Mobile) trinity linkage, cut through various layers of bureaucracy, ensuring no leakages in money transfer as it reached the bank accounts directly without any mediator. Through the JAM linkage, government also saved Rs. 90,000 crore till March 2018 by eliminating duplicate, non-existent and fake beneficiaries. As the then Finance Minister Arun Jaitley said in January 2019, "These savings can fund three schemes the size of Ayushman Bharat."

His non-corruptible image further strengthened, Modi launched a frontal and vicious attack on the opposition. Calling them Mahamilaavat (mega adulteration), Modi would go on to tell the massive crowds who came to hear him, "They have all ganged up against me as I have finished all their shady businesses and now investigation agencies are after them. They hurl innumerable abuses at me, but it is the people who will give them a befitting response." He would go on further and say, "I have challenged these mahamilaavatis. I have made no money, built no farm houses or shopping malls for myself, bought no cars and have no accounts in foreign banks, have never dreamt of riches and never robbed the poor." The point would drive home!

His muscular policy against terrorism and Pakistan was an instant hit. Surgical and air strikes would get huge applauds of approval from the crowds everywhere he went. On Balakot, he would describe the sequence with great elan, "They did not know where I will come from. Will I come from the ground or from under the ground, but I flew from the sky above and hit them," and the whole crowd would go berserk with chants of "Modi, Modi".

In contrast, Rahul's credibility was in a huge deficit. He never held any responsible government position in the past and hence had nothing much to show for in terms of performance. Moreover, being a scion of the family that headed the party, Rahul had to shoulder accountability for the scam-ridden UPA government, which had gone into complete policy paralysis, especially in its last term from 2009 to 2014.

From 2014 to May 2018, Congress lost most of the state elections, barring one odd state. So they really did not have much to show in terms of performance that could clearly differentiate them positively vis-à-vis BJP/NDA government. They were able to form a government in Karnataka in May 2018, but it turned out to be a big drama. There was constant in-fighting and distrust amongst the partners, i.e. Congress and JDS, which was being played out openly, leaving governance in shreds. As a result, the government reputation was tarnished beyond repair. Eventually, that government was to fall post general elections 2019.

In December 2018, Congress won Rajasthan, MP and Chhattisgarh, but schism between the young and old was very apparent in Rajasthan and MP. The other big blunder that all the Congress and indeed many of the opposition state governments committed was, dilly-dallying and delaying on implementing the central government welfare schemes like PM-Kisan and Ayushman Bharat, etc., in their respective states. Modi took a more than full toll of it, going to the town, telling people how their respective state governments, just because of their opposition to Modi, were denying them of benefits announced by the central government. He saved his best for Didi (Mamata Banerjee). He called her

Speed breaker Didi for being an obstacle in implementing central schemes as she could not levy *tolabaji* tax (extortion tax) on them. Modi was referring to the cut a lot of TMC officials and leaders were allegedly extracting from people for providing welfare benefits offered by local government schemes.

Mamata Banerjee, one of the key aspirants for the PM role in 2019, was making the headlines for all the wrong reasons. The Sarada and Narada scams were taking a heavy toll on her and her party's reputation. Her alleged strong-arm tactics were not really endearing her to the people and the political violence and killings in Bengal – especially during the panchayat polls – shocked the whole nation. So much so that the Election Commission had to spread out voting in general elections 2019 across all the seven phases in West Bengal. People also did not appreciate her for not allowing immersion of idols on Vijayadashami as it coincided with Moharram procession, along with her announcing a monthly stipend to the Muslim clergy, both of which was being seen as appeasement politics.

The NYAY, minimum basic income scheme for 20% of the poor of India, suffered from the same credibility issue, given the fact that Congress's record with poverty alleviation programmes has been extremely patchy. People have not forgotten the 'Garibi Hatao' slogan of Indira Gandhi in 1971, which she successfully encashed but delivered little on the ground. Successive Congress governments continued to ignore the plight of the poor, by continually announcing schemes, which would only remain on papers. The schemes that were implemented would suffer from huge leakages and only a trickle would reach the poor. In that backdrop, announcing another pleasing scheme during elections did not hold much credibility.

The scheme also did spook the middle classes and brought back memories of inflationary economy as well as high taxes whenever Congress is in power. Indeed, there was a below the carpet campaign to drive home the point that the middle classes, either directly or indirectly, will eventually have to bear the burden of NYAY, which apparently took them further away from the Congress.

On top of it, when enquired about where the money is going to come from, Congress spoke in different voices. While Chidambaram gave an obscure answer of 'efficient tax management', Sam Pitroda, overseas Congress chief, said the middle class would have to bear some responsibility. On the other hand, Rahul, who was on a completely different tangent, went about telling people from rally to rally that money was going to come from the pockets of the likes of Anil Ambani and other rich people whose coffers were filled brazenly by Modi.

Hence, Congress's reputation of driving policies triggering inflationary economy and taxing the already taxed even more, hurt their ability to convince the people of India. Conversely, by presenting a half-baked scheme, Congress had given a huge opportunity to their adversaries, to hit them at their weakest point.

Maybe Rahul missed a trick or two with NYAY. He could have co-opted the scheme with the opposition and launched it as a scheme from Mahagatbandhan. Not only would the scheme have carried a higher credibility, but it could have also acted as a magnet to bring the opposition together in a manageable way. Rahul's magnanimity could have won him a whole lot of respect with the opposition leaders and they may have finally come around to rally behind Congress. Opposition parties – eventually going their own separate ways after expressing clear intentions of coming together on many occasions, throughout the five years of Modi Sarkar – would have further eroded their credibility. It would have also been a huge disappointment and a loss of morale for the anti-Modi forces.

Hence, the opposition promised much but delivered little. Their egos came in their way of putting up a joint fight against Modi, which put to rest any real hopes that their followers might have had. Rahul did not really have any achievements to his credit to show; rather, he had to carry the past burdens of the discredited UPA regimes. His promise of NYAY suffered due to Congress's poor past track record, negative reputation and lack of preparedness, and made people wary of it. Congress as well as the opposition did not help itself by setting up a less than inspiring record in a few state governments that they ran between 2014 and 2019.

On the other hand, Modi pitched his corruption free governance, development and achievements on national security front to the people of India. Citizens seemed to agree with that on the ground level and a general refrain amongst the voters was to give Modi one one more chance. By 2019, Modi had enhanced his credibility even further and he leveraged that to build acceptability with the people for an even more ambitious future vision for the country and its citizens.

# 19
# Connect with People

When Bapu returned to India in 1915, the Indian National Congress gave him a rousing reception, hoping to utilise his experience from South Africa to help Congress in setting the future course for India. Instead, he got down to the task of improving sanitation by cleaning toilets, fighting against untouchability and removing day-to-day, existential challenges of poor Indians as he uprooted himself and lived amongst them for years. He travelled extensively throughout the length and breadth of the country, mostly in third class compartments of trains to get the pulse of India. Through this approach, Bapu developed a strong connect with people across India. He leveraged this connect and convinced them to stand up for their legitimate rights against the powerful British Empire.

Nearly a century later, in August 2014, a head of state would stand on the ramparts of Red Fort, expected to set a strategic direction for the future for a strong and progressive India, but he spoke of building toilets and doing something about the worsening situation of sanitation throughout the country. He instantly connected with millions.

"Friends, I do not want your kids to live in poverty. I want to change this, and I will be able to change this as I have come from you only. I have seen my mother inconvenienced because of a lack of toilet in the house and discomforted because of a lack of gas connection. I have seen ceilings leaking and I have felt all your pains myself. I know what needs to be done and I shall do it," said Modi during his election campaign in 2019. This was a great example of showing empathy and he instantly connected with each and everyone in the crowd. Modi's disadvantaged background had become his biggest advantage!

Just being an orator par excellence is not good enough. Unless a leader's brilliant oratory is backed by exemplary deeds, he would really sound hollow. However, if he has matching deeds backing him, if he walks the talk, it would automatically bring the confidence and conviction in his voice, demonstrate his genuine intent which would instantly connect him with the people. That is the mark of an authentic leader. Authenticity is a great enabler for a leader to connect with people almost instantly. The genuine anger as well as resolve that writ large on Modi's face when he roared "*Ghar me ghus ke maarenge*" would have sounded and looked hollow if it were not backed by the surgical and Balakot strikes.

Modi held more than a hundred rallies, and at every place, he added a local flavour, which helped him better connect with the locals. When he went to Udaipur, he would invoke Rana Pratap; when in Bengal he would appeal to Bengali pride and say, "What Bengal does, the whole country follows". When he went to Balia, UP, he paid rich tributes to Chittu Pandey, a freedom fighter also known as Sher-e-Ballia.

It would not stop at just this. He would go on to raise local challenges, which people could immediately relate with and then go on to lay bare the solutions the government was working on to overcome them. Thus, in Bihar he referred to a video conference he had with the Bihar youth who told him how because of easy availability of internet, they no longer needed to go to Delhi for coaching classes. In Kannauj, UP, he would talk about developing potato clusters and building cold storages. Wherever he went, he would first start greeting the crowd in their own language and would go on further to say a few more sentences in that language, much to the amusement of the audiences, and endearing him to them even further.

Modi demonstrates a range of emotions and does it with élan, as well as with authenticity rarely seen. Behavioural experts will tell you that the ability to display emotions and share emotional experiences with people is the most effective way to connect with people. However, it has to be genuine, otherwise people will quickly catch fakery and the whole exercise would prove counter-productive. Genuineness can only come if you are well aware and on top of the ground realities. Modi's ability to connect with a diverse set of people across the country is truly legendary. Modi is able to do this after years and years of *pravaas* (moving from place to place) as a Pracharak (promotor) during his days with the RSS initially and then as a BJP worker. He would embark on these social service or party work missions from one small town at one end of the country to another village at the other end, spending the nights at homes of sympathisers or *swayamsevaks* (volunteers), sometimes even living out of people's garages. He understood the scents and smells as well as the pulse of India very well.

Engaging with thousands, and sometimes even lakhs in your audience is an art, which Modi possesses in abundance. He has the uncanny ability to quickly gauge the mood of the audience and engages with them by asking them a question, the answer to which he already knows. For example, on surgical strikes, he would go on and ask, "Tell me, am I on the right path?" The audience would say, "Yes".

"Are you happy?" "Yes" exults the crowd, cheering and clapping.

In this day and age of digital technology, Modi was the pioneer amongst politicians to latch on to digital media platforms. He is ubiquitous on social media, whether its Twitter, Facebook or NaMo App. He is the most followed political leader on Twitter, second only to the US President, Donald Trump. He did video conferencing with millions of booth level BJP workers all across the country, galvanising and motivating them. He took his connect with the people to the next level with his quintessential Mann Ki Baat (talk from the heart), where he talked his heart out to people on day to day problems, and provide solutions and ideas on how to overcome them. He also utilised that opportunity to share some inspiring life stories of people living across India.

Compare that with Rahul, and the difference is clear. Born in the first political family of India meant a life of immense protection and seclusion. Unfortunate assassinations of his grandmother and father further tightened the security ring around him, resulting in restricting his social interactions even further. He went to the elitist of schools, large part of his schooling was at home and higher studies were mostly abroad after which he remained there for more than a decade. He is supposed to have returned to India around 2002.

He was elected as a Member of Parliament (MP) in his very first attempt in 2004. Someone in Congress eventually realised that he needed to connect with people and get a better understanding of India, and in 2008, he embarked on 'Discover India' trips as popularly termed by sections of media at that time. Some would say that it was too little too late, that it should have started much before he even entered the parliament. Some said that he was kick-starting the election campaign for 2009 general elections. Be that as it may, such overnight orchestrated and sanitised trips, where one parachutes down to a forlorn poor family in some corner of India, under the protective eye of a massive security cordon and intense glare of the media, does not really help to build a connect. One needs to live, eat, sleep, walk and work with the common people over years, in a natural way and without any fetters or restrictions to really understand the soul of India.

This is one of the other big drawbacks of being born in a ruling political dynasty where one is declared as an heir apparent even before one is born. Over a generation or maximum two, due to all kinds of restrictions and constraints, security being only one of them, the dynasty loses connect with people and, hence, with reality too. They become completely dependent of their darbaris or KMG, who become the dynasty's eyes and ears through which it sees the world.

Rahul's speeches during the 2019 general elections was a standard template used across the length and breadth of the country as he went around addressing rallies. Moreover, it certainly does not help that Rahul is not a great orator either. His speeches were fairly mechanical and transactional. They were to the point and precise. There was hardly any display of emotions, apart from hatred for Modi/BJP/RSS. Very little, if at all, of compassion, humour, disappointment, regret or even sarcasm and, of course, love! It is ironic that while Rahul so often spoke of having nothing but love for Modi, it never really was evident. On an average, Rahul spoke for nearly half the time that Modi spoke per rally. Rahul took on to social media very late and it appeared reluctantly, never really utilising the full gamut of its offerings. In fact, his IT cell was mired, needlessly, in some controversy or the other a bit too often.

Rahul or for that matter any political leader has miles to go before they can ever hope to catch up with Modi, if at all, when it comes to connecting with people.

# 20
# Lead by Example

"There goes the *fakir* (holy person who has nothing of his own) in a loincloth," people would refer to Bapu lovingly. He shunned his clothing to identify with the millions of poor masses of India living in destitution. If he had to lead them, he had to become like one of them. If someone had to go through pain, he would be the first one to take on the pain. If they were to starve, he would himself starve before any one of them. If he were to preach non-violence, he would be the first one to practise it, and to uphold that, he would always be the first person to go bear the atrocities of the imperial forces. A man of few words, he would finally go on to say, "My life is my message". The world will rarely see a better example of a leader who led by example.

24 January 1992: "There are posters plastered at Lal Chowk. It is written on the walls that whosoever has had his mother's milk should unfurl the tricolour at Lal Chowk and if he is able to go back alive, the terrorists will reward him. I want the terrorists to open their ears and listen, that day after is 26 January. Just a few hours are left. It will soon be decided at Lal Chowk, who has had his mother's milk," said Modi.

At that time, M.M. Joshi was BJP President and militancy in Kashmir was at its peak. Joshi had announced that he would unfurl the tricolour at Lal Chowk, Srinagar on Republic Day, 1992 at the culmination of his Ekta Yatra from Kanyakumari to Srinagar. Modi was the convenor of this yatra and had conceived, planned and organised this Yatra. The militants were furious; they threatened and dared Joshi to unfurl the flag. That was the context of Modi's speech. Two days later, braving all odds, Joshi unfurled the flag with Modi right beside him, undeterred and unfazed. The 56-inch chest was visible then too!

Modi is a man on a mission, who literally works round the clock, 365 days a year, without any break, including the weekends. It is a known fact that he hardly sleeps for three to four hours a day. On almost all major festivals, he would go to the most difficult terrains on the border and spend quality time with the jawans, boosting their morale. Any soldier or security personnel would love to work for a PM who leads from the front, is ready to risk his life for the sake of the nation and is spending every minute of his life in the selfless service of the nation. When you walk your talk, you demonstrate sincerity, which helps you command respect of people.

His life is an open book. He renounced family life very early in life and since then he has either been devoted to social service through the RSS or to party work with the BJP, moving on to being the Chief Minister of Gujarat and eventually the Prime Minister of India. He did not even have a bank account and was forced to open one when he became the Chief Minister of Gujarat as his salary had to be deposited somewhere. That was when he was well over fifty years of age. Prior to that, he was literally moving like a fakir, from one place to another. Nothing has changed materially for his mother or his extended family for the last so many years since he has taken up office. His brothers continue to do odd jobs as they did earlier before Modi took public office, and their families too live ordinary lives. No out of turn entitlements have accrued to them by virtue of Modi being the PM or when he was the CM of Gujarat. There is not even a single paisa corruption charge on him ever since he has assumed public office.

In addition to that, he has ensured no scams happen in ministries under him. Modi critics complain that he has a dictatorial style and all his ministers are constantly under surveillance. PMO is regularly overseeing the works of various ministries as a big brother, is another charge thrown at him. Well, a degree of monitoring is necessary at all levels. You do not want a situation like UPA when there was no oversight at all and we had a dime a dozen scams. Similarly, PMO being the apex office has to oversee and ensure all ministries deliver as per quality and timelines. We do not want another policy paralysis phase, where things did not move and there was no accountability to deliver. A common law abiding citizen appreciates the accountability that PM has brought in the government. How often in private conversations during yesteryears we used to lament the state of government administration and exclaim, "This country needs army rule to set things right!" Well we did not ever mean that literally. In effect, what we meant was that we needed a hard taskmaster and it seems we got one now.

Hence, when he famously said, "*Na khaunga aur na khane doonga*" (neither will I take any bribe and nor will I allow anyone to take bribe), people knew he meant business. And he has proved true to his words. Law-abiding citizens and taxpayers trust that he will utilise the resources of the country optimally and ethically. It is for that reason that millions of Indians willingly gave up gas and railway subsidies on his one call, illustrating people's unflinching faith and trust in him. The last time before this when an Indian premier made a call and people willingly abided by was in 1964 during the Indo-Pak war when there was shortage of food, the then PM Shastri made a call urging people to sacrifice one meal a day. Of course, he ensured that he and his family did that first.

Accountability is not restricted just to the ministers, but goes right down to the level of MPs and MLAs. For 2019 general elections, BJP did extensive surveys across all constituencies to gauge the mood of voters on their sitting MPs. In addition, feedback was taken from other stakeholders too and basis the inputs received, BJP denied tickets to more than 40% of their sitting MPs. This is unprecedented in Indian politics. It is a huge risk to change sitting legislatures as they wield enormous influence over their party structures and workers in their respective constituencies. Critics claim that this proves that BJP is a one-man show. Only Modi matters, they argue. Well, if that were the case, then why change the sitting legislatures and put the local party dynamics at such a risk? They would have anyway won because of Modi. The point is it is not about a leader; it is about a clear intent. Modi's actions have sent a clear message on his intent down the line – perform or perish!

He led the Swacch Bharat Abhiyaan from the front and was one of the first one to pick up the broom to clean the streets. It probably came very naturally to him, as his whole life prior to assuming public office, he would have been fairly accustomed to personally taking care of his daily chores and keeping his immediate surroundings clean and sanitised. Change Management experts will confirm that his personal engagement in the whole programme enabled a mindset change in the people so difficult to achieve in such a short span.

Whatever Modi says, he clearly shows that he would practise that himself first. He leads from the front and people appreciate that and follow him. He is able to make people work hard, as he works the hardest!

> *Happiness is when what you think, what you say and what you do are in harmony.*
>
> – Mahatma Gandhi

Way back in ancient India, there was a famous embrace, when a younger brother went to the forest to meet his elder brother, who was banished from his kingdom just a day before he was to be anointed as the crown prince. He was denied by the guile of his stepmother. As soon as the younger brother came to know that the deserving brother had been banished in his absence, he immediately rushed to the forest to get his elder brother back to the kingdom and have him assume his rightful place. As they met, they hugged each other lovingly and that moment is etched in our memories as "Bharat Milaap" (meeting in exile of Lord Ram and his younger brother Bharat).

Then there was another much talked about hug in the seventeenth century between Afzal Khan, a chieftain of Emperor Aurangzeb, and Shivaji Maharaj, Aurangzeb's sworn enemy. A meeting was arranged to end hostilities between the two forces. After the formal introduction, Afzal Khan asked for a hug from Shivaji as a gesture of friendship. While hugging, Afzal drew out his hidden dagger, but Shivaji had an inkling about his designs and pierced Afzal with his knucle-duster. It was a treacherous hug, which proved fatal for Afzal Khan.

Then, there was the most publicised hug of our times. A crowned prince of a party, which believes that the throne of India is their birth right, forced a hug on a chaiwala who they believed had usurped the throne by hoodwinking the people of India. The chaiwala was perched on the throne in the court, when the crowned prince hugged him and he was taken unawares, as indeed everyone present there. Rahul, after hugging Modi went back to his seat and was immediately caught winking at one of his colleagues sitting close by. The pretence was exposed. One would not need much of an imagination to ascertain which hug it resembled most – Bharat's or Afzal Khan's.

The issue is that people get an impression that what Rahul thinks, what he says and what he eventually does, are vastly different. Rather than providing clarity, it creates a lot of ambiguity and confusion in the minds of the people. Rahul says that he has nothing but love in his heart for Modi. Yet he goes around the country hurling choicest of abuses on Modi. The rage in his voice and hatred on his face are very evident as he goes about criticising Modi.

Moreover, Rahul's biggest pitch questioning Modi's integrity on Rafale sounded hollow in the backdrop of him and his mother, Sonia Gandhi, being out on bail on serious charges of tax evasion and allegedly unlawfully usurping an entity in National Herald case. On top of it, there are serious charges of land grabbing against his brother-in-law, Robert Vadra, who has allegedly exploited his family connections to get some sweet land deals and is being investigated by investigative agencies. In such a scenario, Rahul accusing Modi on corruption in Rafale, that too without any proofs, sounds like Duryodhan giving a sermon to Yudhisthir on Dharma. Rahul had launched his Rafale jet during Gujarat elections to bombard Modi with corruption. Instead, it turned out to be a boomerang, which came back and hit him and his party.

To top it all, to launch an aggressive campaign 'Chowkidar Chor hai' while not even having any shred of evidence against Modi was a big blunder. The Comptroller and Auditor General (CAG) gave a clean chit, the Supreme Court too gave a clean chit, and in fact, Rahul had to offer an apology to the Apex court for falsely attributing Modi-is-a-thief charge to Supreme Court. All the opinion surveys were saying that it is gaining no traction with the public, yet he continued with it. Modi latched on to it and countered it by launching his own 'Main bhi Chowkidar' campaign on 25 March 2019. It was a high decibel campaign co-opting every section of the society as a key stakeholder in building the nation. One could clearly gauge that it gained a lot more traction that the opposition's counterpart. It was Modi's Bali effect working again.

The other smokescreen that the Congress party has created by appropriating and exploited terms like secularism and unity in diversity, can no longer hide the real intentions of the party – of exploiting these concepts opportunistically, with the sole aim to grab power at any cost.

Take for example secularism. On the one hand, Rahul goes on an aggressive temple-hopping spree during elections and displays his batch of a proud devout of Lord Shiva. On the other hand, he says that Congress is a party of Muslims. If you claim to be a torch-bearer of secularism, why play the religion card at all? You cannot be everything to all the people all the time.

There are multiple different and divergent paths towards a goal. One has to make a choice and when one path is chosen, it invariably excludes the other paths. This means that you miss folks on other paths, but hope that in time you will be able to convince them and eventually get them over to join your path. Bapu chose the path of non-violence, which meant that he had to give up on, rightly or wrongly, freedom fighters like Bhagat Singh and Subhas Chandra Bose. Modi adopted a muscular policy against Pakistan, which meant that he had to give a befitting response to them for Pulwana attack. It was a huge risk, but you cannot compromise on your chosen principle, no matter what price you may have to pay, even personally. Under the Congress party, the meaning of the word secularism has degenerated to minority appeasement as rightly claimed by BJP.

In the name of unity in diversity, it seems Rahul and Congress and indeed most of the opposition parties are not averse to fanning fissiparous tendencies. Their open support to forces who shouted slogans of the tukre tukre gang is just one case in point. Their stand on surgical as well as Balakot strikes mirroring that of Pakistan is another example. In our parliamentary democracy, all parties including the opposition have always stood behind the government on foreign policy issues. This, perhaps, is the first time that we are seeing such a fierce criticism of the government and even the armed forces by the opposition that is helping the enemy's cause.

Rahul's elite status and lifestyle makes it difficult for the poor as well as the silent aspirational class of India to relate with him. After all, he is a person who, proverbially saying, has moved from the lap straight on to the throne, without having assumed any administrative responsibilities. He has neither shown any keenness to shoulder one despite ample opportunities to do so, giving an impression that he was avoiding public scrutiny. Hence, he has earned for himself the title of a reluctant politician. 'Avoiding' and 'reluctant' are words that never inspire confidence. A leader cannot afford such words to stick to him.

While admittedly, he showed some spunk to take on Modi, his ability to work continuously on a sustained basis is a big suspect. He continues to leave for undisclosed foreign locations every now and then. Well, while he has complete right to his privacy, lesser the transparency of public figures, higher the risk of getting their images dented. Especially when your opponent is perpetually at play, you leave the ground for a break at your own risk.

Congress sympathisers claim that Rahul being young, appeals to the youth of the country. Let us explore that more objectively. In Rajasthan and Madhya Pradesh, when presented with an opportunity of promoting youth-power, they chose the old warhorses. Both deserving youthful candidates within the Congress – Sachin Pilot and Jyotiraditya Scindia – were sidelined. Rahul was eons behind Modi in adopting social media. While Modi has a way with latest gizmos, Rahul does not really show much of an inclination. The way Modi utilised social media in reaching out to general public, youth and party workers, Rahul did not utilise even half of that. In this multi-polar world, Rahul and Congress want to continue to harp back on its policy of non-alignment of yesteryears (their election manifesto 2019 mentions it). You cannot just blindly keep on going back to policies adopted by your forefathers. When you are living in a time warp, your age does not matter. And when you have someone like Modi as your opponent who has a dare to dream approach, a daringstyle and an attitude of a digital native, there can be no prizes for guessing who the youth will support.

There are quite a few specific attributes that go in building trust as far as political parties and leadership is concerned.

However, the four aspects covered in this book – clarity of higher purpose, credibility, connect with people and lead by example – are broad enough to encompass all factors that impact trust. A consumer insights firm, TRA Research, conducted a brand trust survey, which was published in *LiveMint* on 31 May 2019. The agency took face-to-face interviews of over 2300 customers across 16 cities between December 2018 and March 2019. It was a comparison between brand trust of Modi and Rahul.

Overall, brand trust of Modi was double that of Rahul. There were overall ten attributes and Modi influenced the voters most on four attributes. Modi scored the highest on commanding respect, which really originates from delivering on your promises and leading by example, where he scored 4 times more than Rahul. The next was demonstrated sincerity – again a sub set of delivering on promises and leading by example, where he scored nearly 10 times more of Rahul. Then came altruism, which comes from your higher purpose, where he scored 9 times more than Rahul. The next was enthusiasm, the source of which again is your higher purpose, where he scored nearly 4 times more than Rahul. On all other six attributes – namely, empathy (higher purpose, connect with people), accepting responsibility (delivering on promises, lead by example), perceived competence (delivering on promises), among others – Modi beat Rahul by a significant margin.

If one also considers various opinion surveys across TV news channels before the elections, they clearly showed that Modi's lead over Rahul was almost double when it came to the leader's popularity. The situation really seemed hopeless for Rahul. A popular slogan getting a lot of traction those days was "*Ayega to Modi hi*" (Modi only will come).

## 21
# Modi versus Rest

The whole opposition would have known that Modi's personal appeal was unmatchable. Yet they went for a concerted personal attack against him. They hit him on his biggest strength, which was counter-productive. Perhaps they thought that by pooling their might together and launching a powerful joint attack, they would break through the strong shield of people's trust Modi had built around himself. It looked like a decent plan; however, there was one big problem. Their weapon, which in this case was each of their own individual credibility, for most was far too weak. In mathematics, if you have numbers less than one, and if you multiply them, the result is further reduced. Something similar happened with the opposition. Their combined credibility in the eyes of the public was woefully low, even lower than each one's individual credibility. People got an impression that all the corrupt are ganging up against an honest person.

When they brought up Rafale, Modi highlighted how a few of the opposition members are roaming around on bail while others had investigations going on against them after he gave the agencies a free hand. In five years, he had brought them on the doorsteps of jail, he said; another term and he would send them inside it. People cheered loudly. On one side, there was just the bogey of Rafale, where not even a shred of evidence existed, and on the other side people saw opposition leaders taking the numerous trips to courts, accused of serious charges, seeking bails. The optics were totally against the opposition.

Further, while the criticism on Modi's class and caste continued on and off throughout his term, a fresh volley of attacks were launched on his caste on the eve of elections, raising question marks on his OBC caste. At one of the rallies, he took a dig at the opposition claiming their sole motto is, "*Jaat paat japna, janta ka maal apna*" (Opposition plays caste politics to thug people of their money). At another rally, he made a few serious remarks – "They ask about my caste. My caste is poverty and hence I am a rebel against poverty." Modi was winning this war of perception.

More importantly, the unintended outcome of these personal attacks on Modi was that the opposition, who never wanted it to be a presidential form of election, made it exactly that. They gave it on a platter to Modi who ran with it, much to the dismay of KMG. All their meticulous planning was going to dust. First, their plan of uniting the opposition did not work, and now Modi was converting this whole election into a presidential one. They could only watch it helplessly. At every rally, Modi never missed driving the point home that it was Modi vs Rest now.

Another last ditch effort was initiated by the KMG where a campaign was launched, reminding the voters that India is a parliamentary democracy and that a voter's duty is to elect the MP for their respective constituencies. That all the MPs who get elected will eventually select a PM. However, Modi was having none of it. He would end each and every rally by saying, "*Saathiyon, aapko kamal ke phool per button dabana hai. Aap ka ek ek vote seedha Modi ke khaate mein jaega*" (Friends, you have to press the button next to the lotus; each and every one of your votes will go directly into Modi's account). It was like signing a direct contract with the voters. He was empowering people by appealing to them that this election was about partnering together, co-creating a new India and emphasised the importance of their role in choosing the right leader in fulfilling India's destiny. Modi would go on to roar at rallies that the choice was between him and the rest. He made it very easy for the people! They decided that this time they would not want to depend on their respective MPs. The so-called experts on Parliamentary democracy may cringe, but this time, the Indian voter felt empowered to choose their own PM.

On 23 May 2019, the general election results were declared. BJP and NDA had decimated the opposition. It was a political pogrom. Out of the 36 states and UTs, Congress drew a blank in half of them, 18 to be precise. In 11 out of the rest of 18 states and UTs, they got only one seat each. They got 60% of their seats, 31 of 52, from just three states – Punjab, Tamil Nadu and Kerala. In the Hindi heartland, they won just six of the 225 seats. Leader of opposition Congressman, Malikarjun Kharge, lost and so did eight former Congress Chief Ministers. Rahul Gandhi lost his family seat of Amethi, though he won in Wayanad, Kerala. His insurance policy worked. It was a wise decision to fight from Wayanad too. He will live, politically, for maybe another hug with Modi in parliament, on another day!

For BJP it was a spectacular result. They had won 303 seats and the NDA ended up with a tally of 353 seats. In all the Hindi heartland states, they got over 50% of the votes. In nearly half of the states, BJP and NDA got more than 50% vote share. In the process, BJP set a record to be the first government to return to power with the highest vote share increase of 6%. In 2014, BJP's vote share was around 31% that jumped to over 37% in 2019, an unprecedented increase of 20% more votes for BJP. Exit polls also showed that nearly one third of the votes polled by BJP were solely for Modi. If you take one-third off the 37% votes BJP won, it will come down to around 25% votes, which was the figure BJP won in 1998 under Vajpayee and is the maximum percentage votes BJP had ever won in a general election prior to Modi.

Truly, Modi magic was at play. Modi, perhaps, had seen this coming as he would go on to say in the final stages of his campaigning that it was clear to him that it was not him fighting these elections, but it were the people of India fighting the elections. Perhaps that is why, as some reports suggested, quite a few BJP candidates were taking their campaigns fairly relaxed; they knew they were riding the Modi wave.

A few days post 2019 election results were announced, the author was travelling through the interiors of eastern UP. In a sleepy hamlet in Kushinagar district, the final resting place of the Buddha, when it was inquired of a peasant as to which party he supported in recent elections, he retorted back, "Don't know about any party or the candidate, we only know Modi."

It was TsuNaMo once again! Modi had defeated KMG at its own game; the unbeaten warrior had transformed 543 cuts into 543 shields!

# 22
# Reading the Mandate

How can a country of competing narratives in literally every sphere, hotly contested by argumentative Indians, not have multiple explanations – some diametrically opposite to each other – when it comes to reading the mandate of a general election. Hence, this book will be incomplete without offering an analysis of its own. The role Balakot strikes played in the outcome had been a matter of an inconclusive ongoing serious debate and perhaps will continue to be so until the next general elections. Let us consider a few facts before trying to unravel this mystery:

Firstly, most of the credible opinion surveys shown at national channels did show a slight bump up immediately after the Balakot strikes, around 15-20 seats, which eventually petered out with the passage of time. Remember the strikes happened a good six weeks prior to the first voting day of the elections and as they say, even a week is a long time in politics. In fact, if you replay the tapes of television debates on election analysis up until the exit polls, almost all political pundits had written off balakot strikes as having any significant impact.

Secondly, looking at a similar example from the past, back in 1999 Vajpayee won the Kargil war and within a month-and-a-half of winning that war, the country went through a general election. Vajpayee came back with the same number of seats, 182 to be precise, as he had in his previous government. In fact, BJP's vote percentage decreased by a percent from the earlier election. We will all agree that Kargil was a bigger victory than Balakot. This example does not indicate a war having any major bearing on an election happening within a close period.

Thirdly, let us ask a question, which changes the frame of reference to provide more clarity. Had Modi not embarked upon welfare schemes, would Balakot strikes have helped him win the election? Or given him a significant number of higher seats? The answer to this question will have to be in negative.

However, it will also be wrong to say that Balakot strikes did not have any impact at all. It clearly brought out the stark contrast between UPA inaction post 9/11 Mumbai terror attack and Modi's resolve and daring post-Pulwama attack by sending fighter jets across Pakistan's international border, bombing targets deep inside Pak's territory and challenging its nuclear threshold. On the other hand, the Congress and opposition questioning the strikes and casting doubts on the strikes did not go down well with the public.

Until the Balakot attack, the surgical strike post-Uri was generally seen as a one-off. There was an impression created that India would not be able to risk another one in future. However, the Balakot strikes went a step ahead and thereby reinforced the belief in the minds of people of India that the earlier strikes were not just one-off but a part of a continuum of Modi's new muscular policy on Pakistan and terror. Through these strikes,

Modi had completely differentiated himself from UPA. While this reiteration of the new muscular doctrine would have brought over a few of the fence-sitting voters to Modi's camp, Congress's soft stance on terror and Pakistan would have weaned away from them a few undecided voters. Overall, without any doubt, the strikes would have boosted the morale of BJP workers and built a momentum in their favour.

However, a different kind of strikes did make a huge difference for Modi and he had started launching these strikes as early as 15 August 2014. He launched his first strikes from the ramparts of the Red Fort against filth and squalor. Subsequently, he launched a series of strikes against poverty, homelessness, financial exclusion, deprivation and rejection. If the missiles were the various welfare schemes, then JAM (Jan Dhan Yojana, Aadhaar, Mobile) trinity were the jets through which these missiles were delivered to the targeted audiences. The corrupt, lethargic bureaucratic set up was overhauled to transform into a sharp, disciplined and efficient force to ensure that jets were in the best conditions and fully geared up to deliver the goods.

While the opposition was bombarding the government with their canards like Rafale, EVMs, award wapsi, institutions being compromised, etc., the Modi force was busy hitting the "geo-tagged" (geo-tagging was made compulsory at every stage of house construction in 'Housing for All' project) targets with precision, accuracy, without any noise, and most importantly, without any leakage! The positive unintended outcome of these strikes was that it broke through caste and class barriers, which paid rich dividend to Modi at the hustings. The poor, cutting across caste divides voted for Modi.

An article published in *Hindustan Times* on 7 December 2019 by Louise Tillin, refers to a research paper, which studied data from the post-poll survey conducted by Lokniti-CSDS to ask whether BJP received electoral benefits in 2019 elections from the welfare schemes. It found that for Ujjwala and Jan Dhan Yojana, upwards of 70% people gave credit to central government. The analysis further suggested that BJP and its allies saw a statistically significant increase in the support among the beneficiaries like Ujjwala, Pradhan Mantri Awas Yojana and Ayushman Bharat and they were more likely to vote for BJP in 2019.

All this talk by political pundits of BJP dividing the sub-castes and pitting one sub-caste against another is hogwash and trying to deflect from the main broad point. For all these decades Congress did precious little for the poor, except for making hollow promises and reinforcing the caste-based divisions to rule over them. Disillusioned by Congress, post-Jaiprakash Narayan movement, a different kind of politics started getting played out, where the poor put trust in leaders who emerged through the movement from amongst their own. However, unfortunately, these leaders, like Congress, played identity politics and further honed it only to fulfil their own personal and family interests. The result was there for all to see – these leaders had built assets worth unimaginable figures. Neither the Congress nor these identity leaders did much for the welfare of the commoners, other than treating them as vote banks. The poor, cheated and defeated again, looked up at the heavens and were finally relieved to get a pleasant surprise from the Modi force. The TV analysts speaking ad nauseam on a particular sub-caste within a caste voting for one party and the other voting for a different party, is just splitting hair. When people start leaving you, the one who are farthest from you in your circle of influence leave you first, and so on and so forth. The point is that caste politics is on a rapid decline.

If one looks at the overall picture and compares to 2014, BJP gained hugely in the east of India with Bengal and Odisha. In south, they won massive in Karnataka and did a lot better in Telengana. They lost in UP, but not as badly as the political analysts were predicting. All opinion polls and analysts were giving the BJP not more than 25 odd seats in UP, certainly below 30 and many even pushed the number below 20. However, BJP proved all pollsters wrong. BJP and allies won 64 seats and lost only nine seats from 2014. Amit Shah's game plan of getting more than 50% votes in UP had worked. BJP had gained close to 8% more votes in UP in comparison to 2014. In December, NITI Aayog released the report on Strategic Development Goal Index 2019. In that, UP had shown the maximum improvement among all states. It improved by 13 points from 42 to 55. Assam, Odhisha and Sikkim showed the next best improvement of 7 points. UP seems to have become the new laboratory for BJP – a laboratory of development. In the rest of the country, the results were more or less similar to 2014.

At his victory speech on 23 May 2019 at the BJP headquarters, Modi remarked, "There are only two castes in India today – one is the poor and the other is made up of those who want to lift them out of poverty."

Modi had not just won the poor, but he got huge support from the other caste too. This other caste consists of the rapidly burgeoning middle class. They also call it the neo-middle class as in the last ten years, it has grown threefold. Some call it the aspirational India and this is also the same silent class which is hyper active on social media platforms where it has found its 'voice'. The reasons why they supported Modi are not far to see.

This class does not want special privileges and neither do they want the elite to get any. They believe in meritocracy. They detest corruption. Since they pay their taxes honestly, they hate their hard-earned money being recklessly blown away by corrupt bureaucrats and politicians. They want the corrupt to be brought to book sooner than later. It gives them a great sense of satisfaction and fulfilment when they see the government utilising the taxes, which they pay, for developing infrastructure, eradicating poverty, for health and education. They want the government to secure India's borders and root out terrorism. They are concerned about the internal security threats and want the government to follow zero tolerance policy. They want an integrated, strong and peaceful India. They want law and order to prevail. They want a healthy and sanitised high growth economy that in turn can lead to quality jobs.

It goes without saying that the Modi government has had a distinctively better track record than the erstwhile UPA governments as highlighted in the earlier chapters as well as clearly affirmed by the people of India in the mandate. National security, which was conspicuously absent from the opposition campaign, got a big thumbs down from the people of India. Islamic fundamentalism is a clear and present danger that the government can ignore only at their own risk. UPA government did a great disservice to the nation by coining a fake narrative of saffron terror and diluting the real war on terror. People gave a befitting reply. Seasoned politician, ex-Chief Minister and a top Congressman Digvijay Singh – who apparently was thought to be one of the key members who were involved in coining the term saffron terror – lost in the election to an absolute novice in politics without any track record whatsoever – Pragya Thakur – by a margin of over three lakh votes. People have clearly rejected the equivalence between Islamic terror and Hindu fundamentalism that the Congress was trying to concoct. Both these need to be dealt with separately, and proportionate to the nature of each threat on its own merit.

Modi came in 2014, riding on high credibility established during his chief ministerial stint in Gujarat, as well as his promise to deliver on development, governance and national security. By 2019, Modi positively penetrated the lives of the disadvantaged in an unprecedented way and changed it for the better at a scale, which has never ever happened before. In doing so, he became the messiah of the poor, the first of the two castes left in India, as described by Modi.

India is a land of seekers. Over the years, people have been seeking out messiahs who would help alleviate their miseries and give them freedom from the tight clutches of poverty. Many came promising to be the one, but their promises were only to deceive. However, that story has changed between 2014 and 2019. Modi has earned their trust and has given them a new hope. Having done so, he has in turn earned their unflinching support to carry out tough reforms of the scale and consequence of the demonetisation. They completely trust his intent and root for him like never before.

On the other hand, his uncompromising focus on development as well as cleaning up of the economy, his non-corruptible ways, his digital and start-up push, his muscular policy on terror and national security, his no-nonsense approach to governance and his relentless push to bring the corrupt to be punished has made him the mascot of the other caste, the one that will help root out poverty. This mandate confirms that Modi has clearly broken the boundaries and gained trust across both these castes – the haves and the have-nots – and both seem to be completely aligned behind him in the march to build a New India.

Last but not the least, we need to decode Modi's Bali effect. In May 2019, a few days before the results were announced, in response to Rahul's comment that he had dismantled Modi's image on Rafale corruption, Modi said, "Modi's image is not created by Khan Market Gang or Lutyen's media, but by his forty-five years of toil." He was really summing up his Bali effect. His forty-five years of *tapasya*, of selfless service, of his exemplary deeds and achievements give him that boon, the Bali effect.

People go by what they see on the ground and not by all the canards that are floated in the air by his opponents, bereft as they are of any proof. His Spartan lifestyle, his exemplary selfless deeds, both in Gujarat and then for the whole nation, and the ability to connect with people and communicate his deeds, are the three key elements of this Bali effect. This is also his X-factor. However, this Bali effect or X-factor also comes with a disclaimer for Modi. Even though he may now be surrounded by all the comforts and luxuries of the world, he has to continue living like an ascetic, persist with his toil, and go on with his tapasya for the people and the country. The moment he goes astray on any of the three elements, he will lose his Bali effect.

# Part IV
# *War for the 'Idea of India' Continues*

# 23
# Where does the Congress go from Here?

Halley's Comet is arguably the most famous comet on planet earth. Its long, beautiful and resplendent tail makes it a marvel that denizens of earth wait to watch every seventy-five years or so. It last visited us in 1986 and is due for another look in 2061. We have another comet visit like situation in a particular part of UP, Amethi and Rae Bareilly – every five years during the election time. News TV channels, terming this visit at par with something like the Halley's Comet, assume this to be a spectacle to watch for the whole country. That's why, all of them singularly focus on this event, as long as it lasts. Perhaps, the Congress as well as the KMG hopes that the whole country is sitting in front of their TV sets, watching this celestial and heavenly phenomenon with their eyes wide open.

In January 2019, Congress came up with its brahmahstra – Priyanka Gandhi. It formally announced her entry into politics as the person in-charge of eastern UP. This time, however, it seemed to be more long term and not just a perfunctory outing. Suddenly the whole media was abuzz with a rush of activity. There was a palpable excitement in the newsrooms all across. Many senior journalists and political analysts seemed to have suddenly got a spring in their footsteps and one could perceptibly sense a new-found enthusiasm and energy in their voices hitherto missing. News studios were flowing with effusive praises. They would fondly talk of how Priyanka not just resembled her grandmother, but had also inherited her natural leadership abilities and connect with people. The underlying theme was "Indira is back" and the message splashed through posters all over Lucknow.

Even before her first election roadshow, her first campaign was to accompany her husband, Robert Vadra, as a mark of solidarity, to the Enforcement Directorate (ED) office for questioning. She then followed that up by accompanying him to the ED office in Jaipur too, almost a week later. Of course, she was accompanied by scores of Congress workers too while hogging media attention. This gave some credence to reports that her sudden entry into politics was to create a perception that Vadra's gruelling enquiries were a result of political vendetta and to play the sympathy card by accompanying him to these sessions.

Nevertheless, media could not seem to have enough of her, and the camera dutifully followed her wherever she went. Her first mega roadshow at Lucknow got live coverage. Next day the newspapers could not help gushing about her. One of the national daily headlines read, "Priyanka roars into UP". What one could say for certain, though, was that during the roadshow, thieves did some roaring business. FIRs were registered for fifty stolen mobile phones during that rally.

Well, on the flip side, the camera following you has some major disadvantages too. With all the media attention, her many faux pas moments also started being exposed. Her political naivety was becoming very apparent as days went by, but she really shocked everyone with her reply to a query posed by a reporter to her on Congress candidates. She disclosed that Congress had selected candidates to cut BJP votes even if they were not in a position to win. To be labelled as a *vote katua* (vote cutter) party is the worst ignominy any political party can face, and here the scion of the Congress party was openly claiming to be exactly that.

Finally, the results said it all. Congress number of seats in UP were reduced by half; from 2, it come down to 1. Congress President lost his family seat of Amethi and Congress's vote share came down from 7.5% to 6.31%. It became quite apparent that the buzz and roar was seen in TV studios only. This also proved a point on how media got things so horribly wrong. All the newsroom talk of the revival of Congress due to Priyanka's entry and excitement on the sets was in marked contrast to the sheer indifference of voters on the ground level! Politically, the dynasty seems to have reached its expiry date mark.

So where does Congress go from here? Tarun Gogoi, ex-Congress CM of Assam's statement, post the debacle may hold some clues. On 18 June 2019, his following statements got wide publicity across media channels. He remarked, "I want to emphasise that we need to study how RSS has expanded through the network of social-cultural organisations in the state. This network has assisted RSS to build mass contact. We know how RSS pracharaks fan out to villages, stay there and establish rapport with the people. What is the harm if Congress embarks on such mass contact sans the ideology of RSS."

The Congress in Assam has set a target of winning 80 out of the 126 seats in 2021 Assam state elections. Gogoi went on to add, "We have to accomplish 'Mission 80'. For this to happen, we all have to work on mission mode. We need a robust mass contact exercise the RSS has. I can take a leaf from the RSS mass contact exercise." Gogoi here was specifically talking about adopting this in Assam, but since these comments came in the aftermath of Congress drubbing in the general elections 2019, he was perhaps indicating to apply this India-wide.

It is all very well to say this, however, there is this one basic problem. The intent! He was saying this with an aim to grab power; his goal is 'mission 80'. Gogoi will be best advised to first look at the goal of RSS. Purity of purpose is most important, especially when you are embarking on a social contact programme. It has to do with the uplift of masses and not to cater to a party's personal ambitions to grab power. RSS continues to work with the same dedication and commitment as they have been working since its establishment back in 1925 –with the aim to 'serve the country and its people'. Their pracharaks go and stay with the villagers, for years together, not with the aim to grab power, but to listen to their problems and to solve them. All these things take a lot of effort, time, dedication, sacrifice and selfless service and one will be able to do all this only if you have higher ideals in mind.

Ironically, another Congressman gave a very similar suggestion, but with the right intent. Way back in 1948, he asked Congress to go back to the root of Indian democracy and work in villages for the most disadvantaged people. He knew that if Congress remained to be a political party, in the trappings of power, the real goal would never be served. Hence, in his dying will and testament on 27 January 1948, just three days before he was assassinated, Bapu recommended disbanding the Congress as a political party and going back to the villages and work for the upliftment of the disadvantaged. Excerpts from Bapu's last will and testament are below:

"Though split into two, India having attained political independence through means devised by the Indian National Congress, the Congress in its present shape and form, i.e. as a propaganda vehicle and parliamentary machine has outlived its use. India has still to attain social, moral, and economic independence in terms of its seven hundred thousand villages as distinguished from its cities and towns. The struggle for the ascendancy of civil over military powers is bound to take place in India's progress towards its democratic goal. It must be kept out of unhealthy competition with political parties and communal bodies. For these and other reasons, the All India Congress Committee (AICC) resolves to disband the existing Congress organisation and flower into a Lok Sevak Sangh under the following rules with power to alter them as occasion may demand."

Then Bapu goes on to enumerate ten rules, primarily defining the role Congressmen will play creating a panchayati model type structure. This note was for discussion by the AICC, and thereafter was to put to vote for passage and adoption. Alas, just like many other things Bapu wanted Congress to do, this too never happened. Bapu's fears turned out to be true. Congress has degenerated to an opportunistic party with a sole aim to grab power totally bereft of ideals Bapu had aspired for the leadership of an independent India. Bapu was the soul of Congress. Once he left, Congress was a body without a soul.

Therefore, what Tarun Gogoi mentioned is a good trigger for a much-needed debate within Congress. To draw Bapu's will out again, dust it and reflect on it. However, can it happen? You can take the soul out of the body, but on this mortal earth, you do not have the powers to put it back in! Having said that, miracles do happen!

There is another thing that can happen. Over a period, especially over the last five years, Congress's politics as well as economics have turned completely left, as mentioned earlier. Right from their opposition to the land acquisition bill, to their espousal of left oriented economic policies, to supporting the tukre tukre gang and the so-called urban naxals, to their attitude towards terrorism and Pakistan, their approach to armed forces, their views not only match but mirror those of the left parties. Above all, Nehru, who had a strong affinity towards Left, continues to be the ideal for both Congress and Left. Hence, it would only be in the fitness of things that both these parties merge. It anyway is better to merge than to collide! Eventually, as Indian polity evolves, we are perhaps moving towards a two-party system. Or maybe since India is so diverse, may not be exactly two party, but it may have two larger national parties – one leaning to the right and the other to the left, and a few smaller regional parties aligning with either of the two. Better sooner than later. That is eminently possible if Congress relieves its dynasty.

That brings us to the million-dollar question: can Congress let go of the Nehru-Gandhi dynasty?

In April 2013, Rahul Gandhi in his first ever address to the Indian industry captains at a public forum compared India to a beehive. This was later onmocked and contested, but one could excuse Rahul for coming up with this analogy for a simple fact that he perhaps viewed the world from the narrow lens of the Indian National Congress. Since this 'beehive' analogy fits in very well with the Congress, with the dynasty being the queen bee, it was natural for Rahul to extend it to the whole country. Rahul, while going deeper in explaining the characteristics of a beehive and mentioned that the comparison ended there because while in a beehive each bee has an independent voice, that was not true for us Indians. Perhaps here again he was speaking from his experience of the Congress party and how its hierarchy worked.

The point is, right from its inception, the Congress has been wired to obey the top authority without questioning. First, it was the British. People like Tilak, who challenged their hegemony, had to face severe consequences. Then came Bapu; and people who did not agree with him had to either leave the party or quietly withdraw. Bapu appointed Nehru as the leading face of Congress. Despite an overwhelming majority of Congressmen against Nehru, they quietly went with Bapu's diktat. Since then, Congress has enjoyed decades of power under the shadow of the dynasty and has been lulled by the myth that dynasty is Congress, Congress is dynasty.

We have all heard of the frog experiment, where it is comfortably placed in a pan with tepid water. As the temperature is gradually increased, the frog continues to be lulled by the prior comfort, unable to discern the subtle change in temperature, till a stage where the temperature reaches a fatal point, but the frog continues in its inertia of comfort, and eventually dies.

Congress's position today is like that frog in the pan.

Even as the mercury rises, it is unable to take corrective action and pull out, continuing to believe in the same myth. Whether the Congress will be able to break the myth and bail out well in time, only time will tell.

So who can help the Congress now?

There is this illuminating story which may have the answer. There was this very smart boy in a school. He used to ask such clever questions that most of the time, even teachers did not have any answers. They grew very vary of him and he used to take pride in that fact. Once a new teacher came to the school who seemed to have all the answers to all the clever questions this boy posed. Therefore, this boy, after a lot of thought, came up with a plan to make the teacher cut a sorry figure.

He caught hold of a live sparrow and held it in both hands behind his back as he went to this new teacher. The plan was that he would tell the teacher that he had a sparrow in his hands and ask the teacher whether it was alive or dead. If the teacher said dead, he would produce the live sparrow; and if he said alive, the boy would immediately twist the neck of the sparrow and show up the dead one from behind his back. Hence, both ways, he would win and finally prove this teacher wrong. It was obviously an evil plan, but the boy could go to any extent to uphold his reputation. All set, he goes up to the teacher and smugly asks that question.

The teacher thinks for a moment and gives a reply with a smile, "Son, it's all in your hands!"

It is all in the hands of the dynasty! To be fair to Sonia, from all reports at that time, she indeed was unwilling to enter politics, but hesitantly agreed to take the baton, to save the Congress in 1998. Today the dynasty seems to be in the same situation again; they need to save the party, but this time, ironically, perhaps by pulling themselves out of it.

Congress is in a crumbling state, leaving a vacuum in the opposition space. But nature abhors vacuum. To revive itself, Congress has either to merge with some other force, break up, or change its leadership. However, the best thing for it maybe to fulfil Bapu's will, though a bit late. But better late than never. If it does nothing, it continues limping the way it is, hoping to use its crutches, the KMG and Lutyen's media and strike Modi at the first mistake he makes. A week they say is a long time in politics, five years is an eternity. Modi is stirring the hornet's nest by taking up age old intractable problems, and anything can happen.

# 24
# The Media Politics

Modi critics would say that Modi won through media management, by muzzling press using state power and through brute money power. However, before we go into considering the above allegations, it is important to first broadly understand how media has evolved and how it is structured today. As we do that, we will simultaneously respond to the allegations raised above.

Take the print news publications first. If one looks at the national English dailies, it would be fair to say that over decades, their approach towards BJP has not changed at all. In fact, ever since the BJP has come to power, their attack on the government has become even sharper, as they continue to be dominated by the left lobby. They always have had a strong left leaning and their newspapers continue to be replete with articles from left intellectuals. If Modi indeed is managing them, then it has to be said, that he is doing one hell of a poor job with it.

As far as electronic media goes, up until the 1990s, Doordarshan was the only news channel on television and it was state controlled. The Congress governments of yore would use Doordarshan as a tool to further their own political narrative, interests and agendas. It was only during the Vajpayee regime in late 1990s and early 2000s that there was an explosion of private news channels in various languages on television. Now, almost all news channels broadly follow more or less similar formats.

The prime time news as well as most of the news, generally follows a debate-based format where spokespersons or political experts across political spectrum, mostly evenly distributed, put across their respective points of view. The anchors may have their biases, but generally, all political perspectives are highlighted in the debate.

The other popular format is the seminars, conclaves, leadership summits or interviews of political leaders. Here too, all political parties and leaders get opportunities to put forth their point of views fairly evenly. Especially in seminars, since the number of opposition parties is larger than the NDA alliance partners, invariably, you have more voices that are anti-government than in favour. This, by the way, would also be true for news debates mentioned in the earlier paragraph.

Finally, the Opinion/Exit surveys which perhaps attract the highest TRPs. Here too we have professional and independent agencies that run these surveys. Invariably, in the last two general elections, none of the Opinion surveys were able to predict the wave like situation in favour of Modi. Yes, in 2019, a couple of exit polls were able to predict the numbers fairly accurately, but those could not have in any way influenced the voting pattern, as exit polls are after the voting finishes. The opinion surveys hold the maximum potential of influencing voting patterns of people, and if BJP was really good at managing media, then wonder why they could never manage these surveys?

Moreover, you see the imprint that KMG and Lutyen's media continue to have across all channels. Some news anchors seem to be a part of them. Sometimes they will be there as representatives of the civil society, who will pick on issues selectively. For instance, they will be extremely vocal during lynchings, but give the issue of triple talaq a pass. Then there are these senior journalists and political analysts, who have no qualms of saying that they are anti BJP (pray what happened to the high ideals of journalism) who, forget praising BJP on any issue, would rarely ever give them a back-handed compliment. Egged by the opinion surveys, which almost always underestimate BJPs performance, they start spinning conspiracy theories to try to confuse the public.

In 2019, most opinion polls showed NDA barely making it to the halfway mark or staying short of it. Suddenly, out of nowhere Nitin Gadkari's name started cropping up as possible consensual PM candidate, in case BJP was to fall short of the halfway mark. Purportedly, Gadkari had a go ahead from the RSS after his alleged meeting with the RSS top brass around the time opinion polls were telecast.

Then there is this famous political analyst on UP who on a TV debate before the UP state elections in 2017 was very convincingly articulating how all his ground reports were telling him that the UP ke ladke Akhilesh and Rahul were going to win. We all know what happened back then. He was back again on TV in 2019, this time convinced that Mayavati and Akhilesh have nailed it, and how BJP would be lucky if they were to get even 25 seats in UP. Well, Mayavati and Akhilesh barely managed to get a few more than half of 25 seats! While this is just one example, there are many such moles across news channels.

These so-called political analysts and senior journalists seem to have an eternal shelf life. Irrespective of how hopelessly wrong they are with their analysis in every election, come next elections, and they are back on the TV, getting a place of pride at the channels. There seem to be no performance parameters for such people. Perhaps this highlights the influence and power KMG and Lutyen's media continue to exert on electronic media!

Now, there is a new beast in town called the social media, that sends chills down the spines of KMG and Lutyen's media. Earlier they could get away with their utterly biased views and no one used to challenge them as they had created a closed and protected media eco-system, totally dominated by their own ilk, which left no scope for an alternate view. Now with the whole digital media space opening up with the advent of social media, this tribe is challenged on each and every word they say and write. They not only are challenged, but totally cogent and objective counter arguments leave them speechless most of the times. Of course, people give social etiquettes a miss many times on social media, but one would always take that as a small price to pay for democratisation of communication.

Social media has given a voice to this silent class of citizens who hitherto had no medium to express themselves. This aspirational India has suddenly been empowered by the social media and they do not think twice before expressing their mind. This voice, which had been listening to an outdated monologue for so many years without really having the opportunity to challenge and call out its duplicitous ways, has got a tool today to provide an alternative perspective which is more relevant and grounded. This is what irks KMG no end, and they are quick to write off this new phenomenon as nothing more than BJP manipulating the social media through hired volunteers. Well, it seems yet again, that they have analysed it wrongly. Or perhaps more likely, they are spin doctoring the fact.

There is this charge that Modi misuses state power to drive away the advertisers and suck away the revenues dry from the channels who stand up to him. Well, everyone knows that just as the customer is the king in other commercial establishments, TRP is the name of the game in media. It is not hidden that the channels who claim to stand up against Modi are the ones drawing the lowest TRPs. The question now is which sound business will play their ads on channels with the lowest TRPs?

Other allegation is that BJP uses brute money power. Firstly, it is only logical that the party in power will have the highest election donations. All this while, when Congress was in power, they were in a sweet spot with regard to political funding. Now since the tables have turned, this money bogey is being raised unnecessarily. Secondly, if money power is such an invaluable key to winning elections, then why is BJP is losing so many state elections?

Another criticism on Modi's doorstep is that it is all about marketing and packaging. Marketing experts will tell you that howsoever exceptional your marketing may be, but a poor product will never sell. Moreover, for us Indians, it's a case of once bitten twice shy. In fact, we have been bitten more than once, what with a dynasty having been marketed and sold to us for a few generations now!

The point is that media, which is the biggest lever for KMG, continued to exert a lot of influence, given how far and wide it has spread its tentacles within various media houses. However, it no longer has the monopoly it had over the narrative as it used to have till mid to late nineties. Due to the availability of diverse private channels as well as alternate mediums, their narrative is being challenged at every step. The myths they had created are being demolished and the illusions they have been conjuring are being broken sooner than they ever had been in the past.

However, it cannot be denied that they will conspire again, perhaps with a plot at a much larger scale for Modi 2.0, a plan with international ramifications.

# 25
# Modi 2.0

It was perhaps the most followed and awaited judicial verdict of Independent India. Once the Supreme Court confirmed the date on which the Ayodhya verdict was to be announced, a palpable tension gripped almost the whole country. Forces were put on a high alert, there were prohibitory orders imposed across many areas and section 144 was imposed in Ayodhya.

Cut to 1950, a mosque built on the ruins of Somnath temple, was shifted from that site and reconstruction of a grand temple started, which eventually was inaugurated in 1951. This happened in the backdrop of a bloody partition, so the wounds were still fresh and yet there was no communal strife, no curfews, no section 144s, and most importantly, no courts involved. The endeavour went off smoothly and peacefully. It was not even that Somnath temple was of lesser significance than Ram temple. On the contrary, it had captured the nation's imagination and its reconstruction was hailed as a mark of India's sovereignty.

So how is it that over the past more than seventy years of Independent existence, having sworn to lofty ideals of secularism, unity in diversity, brotherhood and harmony, yet the current communal relations between Hindus and Muslims have come to such a pass. We need to go back to the British period to understand this. The main purpose of British was to rule but for a hand full of people. It was difficult to rule over such a vast and diverse population like India. Any insurgencies would have taken a huge toll on British resources and a sustained rebellion could have ended their rule. So in order to keep us subjugated, they had to break us psychologically, demoralise us and destroy our pride so that we never rise against them.

In order to do that, they created a myth, and it went like this: Indigenous Indians were a bunch of uncultured and illiterate losers who lost all their wars. It is actually the outsiders, who brought progressive ideas and thoughts, knowledge and governance for the good of the country and its people. To reinforce this myth further, they distorted our history, adopted silence on our rich cultural heritage and erased victories of our indigenous heroes while overplaying the victories of invaders over us.

Unfortunately, in post-Independence India, the then government – with the help of eagerly compliant left leaning historians – further sanitised (a euphemism for distortion) our history, and ugly events like oppression, atrocities and religious persecution perpetrated by despots in the medieval past were erased ostensibly with the objective of avoiding bitterness between the two communities. It was a big mistake.

We have learnt with experience that the first step to building trust and reconciliation is to accept rather than deny or be silent. This historical silence ended up creating numerous historical fault-lines. So now, for example, we are in a situation where Aurangzeb is great for a section of people, while he is a despot for the other section; ironically, both are right. One section is going by fact, while the other is going by the myth which has been created and institutionalised by the state itself. That way, it is an even bigger fact.

There are numerous such conflicting historical narratives, which have further aggravated the civilizational wounds and have widened the schism and mistrust between the two communities. With the passage of time, rather than defusing, the positions are hardened as the wounds go deeper, leading to worsening of the situation, making it more difficult to reconcile. A recent case in point is the serious conflict between Armenian people and Turkey. The latter is in denial and refuses to accept the genocide perpetrated on Armenians by Turkey's Ottoman Empire in the early twentieth century, leading to a huge conflict between the two today.

Contrast that with what President Nelson Mandela did at the end of Apartheid in South Africa. He constituted a Truth and Reconciliation Commission to investigate into apartheid atrocities and crimes, not with the view to punish the guilty, rather his goal was to reveal the truth about white atrocities and give a general amnesty in order to make a fresh start on a clean slate. Consider what Mandela did in the light of the silence of our historians and the state, on atrocities committed by certain rulers in the past for centuries, and you realise the enormity of that historical blunder.

Forget about identifying innovative ways to reconcile, a blow to trust between communities was dealt by the state meddling in religion. The then Congress regime's reversal of the Shah Bano verdict given by the Supreme Court and subsequently state's presiding over the Shilanyas at Ayodhya resulted in public outburst of surcharged emotions, hitherto pent up, resulting in the very unfortunate and shameful incident of the demolition of the Babri Mosque. This led to a complete breakdown in trust, not just between the concerned communities, but also between the communities and the state. Experience tells us that the moment politics enters the domain of the gods, battle lines are drawn and stakes increased to such an extent that no party wants to give even an inch, as the consequences could be dire, even fatal. That perhaps was the reason why, when discussions started with the negotiation committee set up by Supreme Court on the Ayodhya matter, before it went into forty days of continuous hearing, parties seemingly were very close to coming to an agreement, but developed cold feet at the last moment when it came to signing on the dotted line.

In addition to these fault-lines, there is a growing threat of Islamic fundamentalism and it is not just restricted to Kashmir. Consider an illuminating interview of Arif Mohammad Khan, now the Governor of Kerala, which he gave to the *Wire* and was posted on YouTube on 27 June 2019.

First, he clarifies that in Quran, only those people who have been victims of aggression, against whom atrocities have been committed or who were thrown out of their homes, are allowed to fight. Having said that, he then goes on to share information on Deoband syllabus for the kids, which mentions that, "*shariat mein Jihaad Deen-e-haq ki taraf bulane aur jo usse kabool na kare us-se jung karne ko kehtei hein*" (In Shariat, jihad is for convincing people to accept Islam, and to start a battle against those who don't accept it). He confirmed that the book from which he quoted, he had ordered from Deoband Saharanpur.

Khan, when asked to comment on Hindu fundamentalism, responded insightfully, saying, 'I cannot talk about others. I need to look at my own house and put it in order. If I do that, my problems will be taken care of. All Muslim clergymen who come on TV raising serious concerns about Hindu fundamentalism are behaving like people whose own house is on fire, yet they ignore that and are worried about a few embers smouldering in the other person's house! Of course, no one stops you from worrying and talking about embers of others, but to do that when you are yourself engulfed with fire seems highly duplicitous.

This finger-pointing has to stop and especially the scholars of each community need to introspect, take ownership and root out violent tendencies within their own. Arif Mohammad Khan's advice is completely in order, not just for his own, but for all communities. Khan also did go on to say that it is only 4% of the kids who are exposed to this curriculum, but the point is that even one person is enough to create mayhem and 4% would still perhaps mean hundreds of thousands. One just wonders whether the outburst of those kids at the Shaheen Bagh, Delhi anti-CAA protests, calling for the blood of Amit Shah and Modi are actually the product of such a curriculum?

Sadly, every religion has radical elements. Most are individuals or small groups that operate on their own at a local level in their own circles. Their influence is small and generally acts as pinpricks in a restricted area. They definitely are a nuisance, but manageable, and are kept under a careful watch. However, here we are facing a threat of organised radicals at a large scale, who in an organised way are injecting poison of divisiveness in kids of their own communities; who in the name of religion are indulging in violence and are funded and morally supported by inimical and fundamentalist forces, not just within, but also from outside. However, very importantly, the community leaders of such organised radical elements will have to be brave and courageous enough to openly and unequivocally come out against them, confront and denounce, just as Arif Mohammad Khan did.

The third critical dimension is Pakistan. Around early 2020, it was widely reported in the press that a few months prior, Pakistan is believed to have hired three lobbying firms in the US. Reportedly, they did not have any lobbying firm for the past six years up to 2019. They have been hired to further Pakistan's interest with the US that may be a euphemism to push Kashmir agenda. We are already seeing anti-India propaganda in Congressional hearings with the liberal left US media being highly obliging.

Hence, you now have a situation, where there are historical fault-lines creating mistrust and Islamist fundamentalism misguiding sections of society. As Modi takes up seemingly intractable generational problems, a vicious propaganda, viewing things only from a Hindu-Muslim binary is underway to cause further disquiet amongst the misguided elements to incite unrest within the country with the view to destabilise it.

KMG seems to be at the heart of this already. It appears the game plan now is to ostensibly dump the moribund Congress, for the time being as it is completely discredited, use it at the most only for their organisation as a support caste. Instead, mobilise the misguided elements and use them as faceless front against the government and create a semblance of anarchy in a few pockets and project it as a country-wide popular uprising. Consequently, it gets picked up a by a few US Congressional representatives as well as a section of the US media. Which then promptly gets relayed back to Indian media as front page headlines, suggesting that now even the world is going against

India, with a view to create confusion and doubt in the minds of the people and destabilise the government.

This is exactly how it played out during the anti-CAA (Citizenship Amendment Act) protests. These protests were organised at around 40 odd universities out of 900 plus universities across India, with only a handful of students from each. Then there were protests across a few cities, there was arson and damage to public property at a handful of places where these protests took place. However, this was splashed across media channels and newspapers for days on end, as if nothing else was happening in India. On the ground though, people were going along calmly with their day-to-day lives. Of course, there were inconveniences around those areas where protests took place, which is only natural. The point to note is that the media response was disproportionate and exaggerated.

Next, we read in newspapers on the front page that at a few Congressional hearings in the US, the Congressional representatives rapped India on CAA and we get to hear of names of people we have never heard of earlier. This is then followed by a set of ex-bureaucrats, of course from the erstwhile UPA regime, getting wide publicity in media for mentioning how India is being isolated across the globe and how advisories are being passed against India. This time it seems to be a battle of perceptions with international ramifications. The basic idea appears to be to tell people that 'look, we kept telling you for the last five years that Modi is communal and dictatorial and you did not listen to us. Now see, even the world is saying that.'

This time, it seems the KMG seems to be back with a vengeance, determined to take the war global, as probably they have found a great ally in Pakistan, taking an outside-in approach with an even more ambitious goal to bleed Modi with a thousand cuts in 2024.

Government will also need to be wary of the nefarious designs of these behind-the-scene forces, whose objective also seems to be to spread fear-mongering and drive a wedge in the already precarious relations between the two communities, given that India is in a tinder-box situation. The lesson from the CAA experience is that in future, on big changes directly affecting communities, government may well give itself more time to inform and prepare the masses. This is necessary to scuttle any possibility of inimical forces unleashing propaganda to try to destabilise the situation.

As Modi deals with these internal challenges as well as external threats, he will have to bring the economy on track for the prosperity of the people and the country, which is paramount. Along with this, he will also have to deal with the international push back, due to the internal challenges as well as India's muscular external policy. In today's times, economic growth is a critical lever in international relations. The higher your economic growth, the more people listen and agree with you.

People will be watching Modi on bringing the corrupt amongst the high and mighty politicians to book. He will have to fulfil his bail to jail promise in this term. Fairly early on in his first term, the idea of fast track courts for the law makers was mooted. However, it seems it did not gain much traction with the Apex court. There should be a renewed effort to institutionalise this mechanism. Politicians are well aware of the sad state of Indian courts where cases linger on for decades and eventually fizzle out due to fatigue. Hence, they exploit that sorry state and indulge in corruption with impunity, knowing fully well that they will not have to bear the consequences in their lifetime. If we can bring them to book quickly, it will have a salutary effect down the line and act as an effective deterrence for babus too, eventually bringing big relief to the hapless society facing the scourge of corruption.

However, the number one agenda, the top priority of Modi has to be – welfare! The promise of housing for all, doubling farmers' income and alleviating their distress must be fulfilled. The new promise of tap water to every home must be delivered. Ayushman Bharat must reach all the intended beneficiaries. Reaching and touching the poor directly was one of the key reasons why people put their trust in Modi. He needs to continue strengthening that trust by delivering on these key promises and people will continue to support him wholeheartedly as he goes about trying to solve the vexed issues the country has been jostling with for decades. His welfare economics will continue to be the key fulcrum that will catapult him back, yet again in 2024, to serve the nation.

# 26
# The idea of India

India, that is Bharat, is a land of seekers. Questions like, "Why do we exist", "Why do we die" and "Why there is pain", troubled our ancestors. So they started seeking answers with a goal to achieve eternal life, knowledge and happiness. They contemplated, meditated hard and through the spirit of inquiry came the awakening. They had gained the knowledge that there is one Supreme Being and a man's goal is to reach him and attain eternal life knowledge and bliss. They also learnt that there are many paths to this Supreme Being and each individual had to discover his own path, just as they themselves did.

After our ancestors left us, their knowledge passed down orally to the generations that followed. Ram and Krishna walked on this earth and set an example for people to follow, through their lives and preaching. Then came Buddha, the enlightened one, and Mahavir who reasoned and convinced scores of people, and they started following the paths shown by these two. So much so, that during the tenure of Emperor Ashoka, Buddhism was the state religion, which probably meant that it enjoyed a massive following.

Then came Shankaracharya who through his practise of debates – which he conducted across the length and breadth of this land – reasoned out and convinced the people, and majority started following the Vedic practises again. Around the same time came Christianity to this land and people embraced it. Zoroastrians too came after suffering from persecution in Persia and people took them as their own.

In the medieval times came Islam and people embraced it. In also came Sufism and its syncretic traditions which resonated with the people of this land and they made it their own. Some rulers indulged in persecution, oppression and forceful conversions, but despite that, the majority followed their free will and continued following the philosophy of their choosing. During the oppressive times came an illumined soul, Baba Nanak, who showed the light to people and many followed him. Sikhism was born. When oppressions continued and severity increased, Sikhs took up arms to protect the weak and oppressed under Guru Gobind Singh.

Our ancestors also taught us not to blindly accept, but reason out, contemplate and create our own path. Or choose to follow a path shown by other only when convinced with it. That's how Krishna came and explained to us the four paths to achieve God – Raj yoga, Gyan yoga, Bhakti yoga and Karma yoga. Buddha came and inspired us to control our desires and meditate. Mahavira taught us the path of renunciation and harmlessness. Christianity and Islam taught us to put faith in god and equality of all people. Nanak preached love for god and serving him through selfless service to humanity. Scores of Sufis and other enlightened beings all across the length and breadth of this land preached their paths, each having countless followers.

While all of them preached their own paths, there were a few things common to all. All believed in one Supreme Being, all preached equality, brotherhood and peaceful co-existence, and all taught love, compassion and service to others.

This then is the 'Idea of India', a land where people believe in the existence of one supreme being, whom people call by different names. They also believe that there are many paths to reach that being, which is the goal of human life, and that each one has the freedom to select his or her own path. All, irrespective of the path they follow, are equal and live in peaceful co-existence.

It is because of this idea of India that over the ages, people gravitated from one religion to another and then back, and so on and so forth. But the key is that they have always had a religion or faith in that supreme being. They also believe that there are many paths to reach that being and that they, through their spirit of enquiry and free will, after listening and learning from great souls, chose the path that they reason is most suited for them. As they go along, they again may choose to change the path, if they deem fit. It is because of this idea of India that religions like Islam, Christianity and Zoroastrianism, which were not born here, were embraced by India.

It is because of this idea of India that even today, we continue to have hundreds and thousands of sects which have branched out from the main religions and preach their own syncretic philosophy, each having multitude of followers from different religions. We have scores of godmen in India with millions of followers, all believing in god, with a goal to seek bliss, happiness, material wealth, knowledge, redemption, meaning of life itself and above all, liberation.

This idea resonates with people across this land. Otherwise, this land is so diverse that at every hundred kilometres, the culture, food, language, clothes, nearly everything changes.

This idea is what unites us. That is the uniting factor of unity in diversity of this land. This idea of India existed on this land when India did not exist in the form it exists today. When India was divided in over five hundred principalities, this idea was the common thread across all those principalities.

It cuts through class, caste, religion and region. This idea is also the one which differentiates us from the rest of the world. Which other nation in this world has given birth to so many religions, embraced so many? Is the most multi-religious, nearly cent percent of the population are believers and yet does not have a state religion? All this is possible only because of this idea, the real idea of India, which unites us and which is our unique identity. This is true Bharateeyata.

As this idea of India or Bharateeyta is universal and believes in equality of all human beings, whether believers and non-believers, we have a place of honour for atheists and agnostics too. Our first Prime Minister was a proclaimed agnostic and despite being a country of believers, we gave him a long reign as a leader of this nation. If you are not convinced, it is fine to be a non-believer. You will continue to be our equal in every respect.

Shashi Tharoor famously said in November 2018, “If we today have a chaiwala as prime minister, it is because Nehru ji made it possible.” Well, the fact of the matter is that Nehru ji became the prime minister because of Bharateeyta, which is also the fundamental reason behind the chaiwala becoming the prime minister later on. However, it is understandable for Shashi to say so, as Congressmen very reluctantly recognise history prior to the twentieth century or thereabouts.

Because Bharateeyta is holistic and tolerant at its very core, it allows you a choice of either to follow the paths of sensory pursuits or go up the ladder of spiritual ideals. So while we have ascetics galore who surprise us with their teeming numbers on occasions like the Kumbh, where they gather in hundreds and thousands, and on the other side we have the colourful celebrations of festivals and foods across the land throughout the year. Just when one would think that these paths, ascetic and sensory, might never converge, it is then that a spiritual guru arrives and in the most unexpected ways, advises his devotees to eat a white coloured sweet for one kind of problem and a brown coloured sweet for another kind. It is due to this idea of India that we see diametrically opposite impulses play out in their broadest expanse possible, in parallel, and in complete harmony. That is why people call this land 'A country of contradictions'. Whatever is true of India, the opposite is also true!

Hence, to clarify further, the three critical elements of Bharteeyta are as follows:

### *Belief in A Supreme Being, Entity, Divinity, Universal consciousness*

India, that is Bharat, is a nation of believers, nearly cent percent people in India believe in some faith, sect or religion. Muslims, Christians and Sikhs believe on one Supreme Being. While Hindus may have a few crore gods, they all ultimately subsume into one Supreme entity, Om. The Buddhists believe in universal consciousness and the Jains believe in divinity.

### *Freedom to choose your own path or create your own path to reach divinity*

This is the reason why despite being a religious country, we are not a theocratic state. Because religion is personal. Each individual has a right to choose his or her own path. We are not secular because this word was added in our Preamble under the cover of darkness of emergency. We are secular because our ancestors passed this belief on to us, and it is in our genes. There were periods when India became theocratic during Ashoka's reign and during the Mughal period; however, theocracy eventually did not survive because the idea resisted it.

There are innumerable examples in countries in the Middle East where conquerors converted the whole populations to their own religions within a few decades. However, that never happened in India, precisely because the people, guided by their principles, fiercely guarded and protected their freedom to choose. Different religions dominated this land at different times and ultimately realised the futility of it all. The people belonging to this land made supreme sacrifices to protect their freedom to choose and Sikh Gurus exemplified that. This aspect is the reason why India is multi-religious; it has thousands of sects and millions of their followers and innumerable gurus of all kinds.

It is because of this thought that even though there are few, but there is space for even atheists and agnostics. However, this idea agitates and rejects any kind of fundamentalism. Whether it is Islamic fundamentalism or from any other religion, this nation will never allow any fundamentalist thought to dominate the narrative. Radicals will always remain on the fringe. In independent India, if unfortunately this thought ever got any prominence, politics triggered it. That is why the people of this nation abhor political meddling in religion. Religion is a private space, it is a contact between god and man and its sanctity must be honoured.

### *All are equal and live in peaceful co-existence*

All the great souls and preachers who walked on this land, irrespective of the paths they taught, had this thought in common – all men are equal and they must live harmoniously with each other. In modern times, the one who taught a lesson of non-violence to the whole world was none other than Gandhi. Non-violence is our ethos, which is why India has never been an aggressor against any nation.

This thought rejects the social hierarchies or the caste divides. Castes were perversions that crept in much later. In modern times, while there have been many social reformers, Gandhi was among the most prominent of them all, who not just fought against the scourge of untouchability, but also went and lived with the most dispossessed and worked for their uplift.

This Bharateeyta is also the message of spirituality to the whole world. This is spiritual because this is only between god and man, and man's quest to reach god. There is no third entity in between. Man can choose to have a third entity, a guru, to reach god, which is purely man's choice. This informs that you do not even require any rituals to perform and advises to look within.

Because India is spiritual, hence it is secular. Spiritualism precedes secularism. When spiritualism was there, secularism did not exist. Spiritualism is primordial while secularism is a modern construct. Spiritualism subsumes secularism. If you believe in spiritualism, you automatically are secular, but the opposite may not necessarily be true. It is this secular idea of India that ensured that during our darkest days and in the midst of orthodoxy, we had great souls like Swami Vivekananda, Shirdi Sai Baba, and the sufis. Fundamentalism and oppression brought in redemption in the form of Sikhism and Bhakti movement. All these great souls that walked tall amongst us preached us equality of all beings and peaceful co-existence. This idea continues to ensure that while these souls are no longer with us physically, they will forever occupy the minds and hearts of millions and millions of habitants of this land and beyond, and their preaching will forever walk tall amongst the lowly rumblings of fundamentalists.

There is another contradiction that amazes many of us, even riles us. While India has such exalted ideals, it is the preacher of spiritualism and claims to be the country of holy men and women. Yet corruption is endemic, moral values are low, a few of the rich are getting richer while millions continue to live in poverty. It is because the modern Indian nation state forgot about spiritualism, the essence of Bharteeyta. Spiritualism that acts as a moral compass also subsumes service to others, selflessness, sacrifice, equality, liberty, love and compassion. In denying itself spiritualism, India gave up most of these ideals.

It is the misfortune of this land that few, especially in the governing class of people, have tread the much-exalted path, the path of selfless service, sacrifice and working for the disadvantaged. The governing class never committed themselves to this idea of spiritualism, and hence never applied it to their functioning. It will be fair to say that the political class in India, failed India. All these talks of socialism, equality, secularism, unity in diversity, over the last more than seven decades has miserably underachieved on almost all counts. It is necessary for a state to have a strong moral compass, which guides it and saves it from going astray on a wanton, selfish and corrupt path.

It is this spiritual path that Swami Vivekananda and Bapu showed, but very few followed. However, today we have a person at the helm of affairs, who is emulating these greats, and working to uplift and empower the millions of downtrodden. He is also charting out a daring path never travelled before by taking up on the thus far intractable legacy problems, one by one. For he knows that till India gets these issues out of the way, it will be difficult to unleash its true potential and gain its rightful place in the comity of nations.

He is working relentlessly to make this nation strong socially, economically and militarily. This fakir (ascetic who lives through alms), hit the national stage with a bang, and when the time comes, will quietly fade away into oblivion.When talking about the inevitability of him moving out of the Prime Minister's residence one day, he had proclaimed, *"Mera kya hai, hum to fakir hein; jhola uthaenge aur chal denge"* (What about me, I am a fakir. I will lift my cloth bag and move on).

But he has miles to go before he can rest. The battle for 2019 may have been won; however, the war for the idea of India continues. A war, not between Modi and the rest, but actually a war between Swami Vivekananda's & Bapu's Bharteeyta and Nehru's misplaced ideals.

*And the war continues...*

# Epilogue

Ever since Modi took charge again as PM in May 2019, much water has flowed from under the bridge. COVID -19 has ensured that perhaps the world will never be the same again and in its wake, China is hell bent on changing the geo-political power equations of the world with its hegemonic pursuits. India is right at the epicentre of both these global events, and it can either take it as a challenge and manage it, or seize it as an opportunity and leverage it. Nationally, while the Congress/opposition continues to be stuck in a morass, Modi government has been working at a feverish pace banning triple talaq, passing Citizenship Amendment Bill, abrogating article 370, announcing a slew of economic, labour and agriculture reforms, promptly setting up a trust that enabled the quick kick-starting of the Ram Mandir construction and much else. All this in little less than one-and-a-half years. With more than three-and-a-half years to go, my mouth salivates at the prospect of writing an even more fascinating sequel to this book post 2024. Time would tell, but it is worthwhile to touch on, briefly, a few critical issues as a curtain-raiser, which are definitely going to be the underpinnings for the election campaigns of all political forces for the general election in 2024.

## *COVID strikes*

COVID-19, an unforeseen crisis – the likes of which the world had not seen for over a hundred years, the scale of which the current generation has never ever experienced – hit the world in December-January 2019. It is difficult to indulge in crystal ball gazing but it will be fair to say that it has changed the world forever in quite a few aspects. Despite the devastation it has brought in its wake, there have been a few refreshing learnings too. Post lockdowns, it was heartening to see nature reclaiming its lost spaces fairly quickly. One could see animals, rarely seen in the dense concrete jungles of the cities, coming out from the nearby thickets, onto the empty streets and even into the residential areas strutting across fearlessly as if on a victory lap after having defeated the human race. It was also a pleasant surprise to note how swiftly the environment could recuperate. Within days of lockdown, people were amazed to see the pollution levels coming down significantly, river waters becoming clearer and cleaner. From cities, there were citings of mountain ranges, which were a few hundred kilometres away, which had not been seen by the naked eye for decades due to pollution.

It perhaps would be worthwhile for the government to consider a fortnight long couple of lockdowns each year for the next few years, given the precarious situation with the environment that the world, especially India, grapples with. Summer holidays are an ideal time for one when all the schools/colleges are closed anyway, and the second could be during Dushehra/Diwali holidays. Industries, the main cause of pollution, and corporate offices should remain shut while essential services could continue. Wherever possible, people should work from home during these lockdowns. Industries could easily plan their inventories in advance, so there are no disruptions in supplies. This is eminently doable and we already have west as an example where mostly the whole of it is shut down during Christmas and New Year, for around three to four weeks.

COVID also has hastened some of the trends that were gradually shaping the world, i.e. digitisation and de-globalisation. India was already on a fast trajectory as far as digitisation was concerned and COVID just hastened that up by quite a few notches. China, the global supply chain hub, was already challenging the rule-based global order, so organisations were looking at de-risking and reorienting supply chains out of China and shifting out to other locations. Post COVID, as China went rogue with its expansionist agenda, the process of de-globalisation picked up further pace.

### *The Dynasty continues...*

Post defeat, Rahul Gandhi resigned as the President of the Congress party in a huff, blaming the senior leadership for not having supported him in directly taking on Modi. Quite predictably, Sonia Gandhi was made the interim President, but there was no doubt of who actually was leading the party. Rahul Gandhi continues to be in the forefront, spewing venom at Modi.

Most of us have heard the fable "The boy who cried wolf", in which a shepherd gathers people around him every time by falsely crying wolf, and when the wolf actually comes, disbelieving him, no on turns up for his help and he gets eaten up by the wolf. Well, Rahul Gandhi is that quintessential boy in Indian politics. He seems habituated of raising false alarms, spewing blatant lies, perhaps the most famous being the vicious 'chowkidar chor hai' campaign. A month or two back, Rahul cried wolf on COVID-19, raising alarm right from acute food shortage to raising baseless concerns on data security concerns on the Aarogya Setu app.

His utterance on Twitter on China issue, taking a jibe at Modi calling him Surrender Modi, other than attracting public ridicule, yet again indicates his visceral hatred for Modi and the fact that he could go to any extent to criticise Modi, even at the cost of harming national interest. Rahul has the right to criticise and even ridicule Modi, but has to be mindful of when to do it. Rather than putting up a united front, Rahul is ridiculing Modi at a stage when our army is engaged in crucial negotiations with the Chinese army on border dispute. Such statements have the potential of giving the enemy an upper hand. Thankfully, people are able to see through such blunders and hence, not many citizens seem to be falling for Rahul's assertions, a pointer to his low trustworthiness.

There are other reasons too for Rahul's low credibility. Consider Jyotiraditya Scindia's exit from the Congress not very long ago. Soon after Scindia's exit, the Congress's youth icon, Rahul Gandhi, who is supposedly a magnate for youth as claimed by Congress, expressed helplessness and publicly wondered why Scindia did not approach him before leaving, when his doors were always open for Jyotiraditya. Indirectly, he put the blame on Scindia. However, Rahul also went on to clarify that he would meet him only for personal reasons and not for party matters.

Hence Scindia, who has been completely occupied fighting a lone political battle in MP for the past fifteen months, should have visited Rahul, not to discuss politics but perhaps to play a game of ping-pong! As that seems to be Rahul's view of what the young leaders in Congress should be pursuing, leaving the mundane business of governance to the old guard. Rahul himself has been shirking away from assuming responsibilities of governance; he perhaps feels it is too early for folks like Scindia too.

Rahul's excuse was that since he is no longer the Congress President, hence no one should approach him for any party matters. Someone who aspires to be the PM, Rahul can abdicate titles and positions, but he cannot wash away his hands from responsibilities and accountabilities. Mahatma Gandhi, after a few initial years, held no position or authority in Congress, but continued to hold sway over the party like no one else, purely based on his personal influence. Moreover, most importantly, he assumed full responsibility of the party, especially when things went wrong.

It is not enough to adopt the surname of the Father of the nation; one needs to imbibe his qualities and emulate him. Far from it, lately, devoid of any new ideas and issues, he has started flogging a dead horse and raising old, beaten issues like Rafale, demonetisation, GST, etc. It is as if the final exams are over and all the students have moved on to the higher class but Rahul continues to revise and raise questions from the previous class!

If Rahul continues to display such an attitude of crying wolf at the drop of a hat, using hackneyed scripts and repeating lies, shirking away from responsibilities of governance and party organisation as well as abdicating accountability while being constantly in a blame-it-on-the-others mode – it is only a matter of time when the proverbial wolf eats up the Congress party.

Recently, a group of twenty-three Congressmen mustered the courage and wrote a letter to the party president asking for internal reforms. However, it proved to be an exercise in futility. The dissent was promptly squashed, members who showed the temerity to ask the question were snubbed and shown their places. Licking their wounds, they were left red-faced claiming they were misunderstood and were at pains to clarify that they had not challenged the authority of the family. Hence, while India may take some while in achieving 'status quo ante' with China at the border, it was arrived at fairly quickly in the case of internal dissent in the Congress party. As mentioned earlier, it is all in the hands of the dynasty!

## *The China Conundrum: Time to think and act big*

> *Those who win every battle are not really skilful – those who render other armies helpless without fighting are the best of all.*
>
> – *Sun Tzu,* The Art of War

The above statement seems to be the sum and substance of the tactics employed by Chinese against India when it comes to the Line of Actual Control (LAC). The salami slicing tactics by China have continued unabated since a long time. They have been creeping westward of the LAC on a sly, without getting into a war with India and without shedding even a drop of blood. India's deferential attitude towards China was obvious and China exploited that to the full. During UPA regime, China reportedly grabbed over 600 square km of land. China chipping away at the LAC and India's passive response possibly gave an indication of its tacit acceptance of China's superiority in the region. Without fighting a war, China's salami slicing and India overlooking it seemed to be the actual 'status quo' at the operational level on the ground. However, that was before Doklam happened!

When India, having given a free hand to its armed forces, pushed back China from Doklam in 2017, it was a tectonic shift, forcing a 'new status quo' in Indo-China border relations. It would have definitely shook China. However, they probably thought it to be a one-off incident. Therefore, after reinforcing resources, in a bid to restore status quo ante, they started with their salami slicing tactics in April-May of 2020. But then Galwan happened; it was Doklam redux. Only this time it was bloody and China suffered much higher casualties than India as per estimates. However, China did intrude in disputed areas, so called no man's land at Pangong Tso, Gogra and Depsang areas.

China's deceitful attitude was on display again. Post Galwan, while the military level discussions to bring peace and tranquillity at the border went on, China again tried to intrude in a few areas in Pangong Tso and Chushul sectors. However, India successfully not only repulsed the Chinese, but also assumed control of a few strategic heights in these unmanned areas, thereby giving the Chinese a taste of their own medicines. Hence, India seemed determined this time to maintain and reinforce its new status quo, which is that India would no longer overlook and allow any transgressions by the Chinese. It seems clear now that their moves to restore status quo ante will be repulsed, even if that means going kinetic, a euphemism for 'war'.

One of the other key tools in China's warfare strategy is PR propaganda. It exploits media to highlight its exaggerated prowess to intimidate opponents to the extent that they lay down their arms even before a shot is fired. Its controlled media then goes on to provide unsolicited open advice to join hands with

China, accept its hegemony and in the process, China gives a guarantee to maintain peace and tranquillity at its borders. It is a script straight out of a Bollywood movie where the big don first bullies the victim and eventually negotiates to provide protection to the bereaved... from his own self, in return for some material considerations. However, as far as India is concerned, it is having none of the Chinese propaganda. In fact, some of the Chinese propaganda videos have been so hilarious that they have adequately replaced the tik-tok videos, which were banned by the Indian government in the aftermath of Galwan.

The other key ploy by China, like a game of chess, is to surround the enemy from all sides, isolate it and eventually defeat it. While chess finds its roots in India, the Chinese seems to have by-hearted the lessons and applied them on us. In August 2020, while the stand-off with India was on, China held a joint meeting with Pakistan, Afghanistan and Nepal, stressing the need to resume its pet BRI projects, in return of which, it promised the supply of COVID vaccines to these countries whenever they were ready. Similarly, China has been building economic relations with Sri Lanka and Bangladesh too purportedly with an eye to checkmate India.

However, in its neighbourhood too, India has played smartly. Recently, Sri Lanka openly stated to have an 'India first' policy and they have even regretted to have gone ahead on their port project with China. India is strengthening ties with Bangladesh and huge impetus has been recently giving to connectivity projects. Nepal, after the recent hiccups, has been reaching out to India. Moreover, of late it has also become a victim of China's transgressions. Pakistan has been successfully isolated and Afghanistan recognised the critical role India plays in its development.

On the other hand, India is hitting China where it will hurt it the most – its pockets. While banning of Chinese apps and strict control on its investments in India, which may not account for much for China, India's decisions have triggered similar reactions across the developed nations, which in all probability will significantly harm China's economic interests in the future.

Moving forward, India needs to start reaching out and form coalitions with China's neighbours like Taiwan, Vietnam, etc., troubled as they are by China's territorial ambitions. It has invigorated the Quad (partnership between India, US, Japan and Australia) and initiated joint military exercises in the region which for a long while were in a limbo.

China has been violating the Panchsheel agreement by instigating our neighbours against us all this while. To top it all, it openly supported Pakistan in its unsuccessful attempt to raise the issue of the abrogation of Article 370 at the UN in 2019. Hence, India must start aggressively raising the genuine human rights violations committed by the Chinese on Uighurs of Xinjiang as well as the Tibetans. India needs to openly and unequivocally support the Dalai Lama's stance on getting religious and cultural autonomy for Tibetans. We must strongly oppose China's brazen meddling in the selection process of Dalai Lama's successor.

Now that the USA has started calling out China as a rogue nation, India needs to seize this opportunity, step up the heat and push for the restructuring of the UN Security Council. Since US has taken such a strong anti-China stance, it is now in an embarrassing position of sitting at the same table as China, as a permanent member of the Security Council. India needs to exploit this unease and build advocacy for a review of China's eligibility as the permanent member of the Security Council.

The world has been asking for key reforms at the UN but a major change happens only when there is a pressing case. A brazen, unethical and rampaging China is that case. India should leverage this opportunity and build a strong case that could help it catapult to a permanent membership at the United Nations Security Council.

If we aspire to become big, we need to think and act big! More importantly, we need to do this to uphold the values of equality, compassion, free thought and expression and human dignity. We need to stop the hegemonic intentions of an unjust neighbour, unequivocally challenge and call out its nefarious designs. Of course, China is bigger than we are, hence we need to punch above our weight and be more agile as well as nimble. We need to leverage our strengths, i.e. we are better in mountain warfare, our Air Force has an edge on the heights, our troops' preparedness is better and morale is much higher than theirs. We need to take the lead in stopping China in its steps. We have the right reasons to do so, we have the just cause to fight for and we know that we will get support.

It is time now for us to show that we have it in us to be a world leader, a Vishwa Guru!

# List of acronyms

| | | |
|---|---|---|
| AICC | – | All India Congress Committee |
| BJP | – | Bharatiya Janata Party |
| BSP | – | Bahujan Samaj Party |
| CAA | – | Citizenship Amendment Act |
| CAG | – | Comptroller and Auditor General |
| CPI(M) | – | Communist Party of India (Marxist) |
| DBT | – | Direct Benefit Transfer |
| DMK | – | Dravida Munnetra Kazhagam |
| ED | – | Enforcement Directorate |
| EVM | – | Electronic Voting Machines |
| FY | – | Financial Year |
| GST | – | Goods and services Tax |
| INC | – | Indian National Congress |
| JAM | – | Jan Dhan, Aadhaar, Mobile |
| JDS | – | Janta Dal (Secular) |
| JDU | – | Janata Dal united |
| JeM | – | Jaish-e-Mohammad |
| KMG | – | Khan Market Gang |
| LAC | – | Line of Actual Control |
| LJP | – | Lok Janshakti Party |
| LoC | – | Line of Control |

| | | |
|---|---|---|
| MLA | – | Member of Legislative Assembly |
| MP | – | Madhya Pradesh |
| MP | – | Member of Parliament |
| NCAER | – | National Council of Applied Economic Research |
| NCP | – | Nationalist Congress Party |
| NDA | – | National Democratic Alliance |
| NIPFP | – | National Institute of Public Finance and Policy |
| NPA | – | Non productive Assets |
| PM | – | Prime Minister |
| PoK | – | Pakistan Occupied Kashmir |
| PWC | – | PricewaterhouseCoopers |
| RBI | – | Reserve Bank of India |
| SIT | – | Special Investigating Team |
| SP | – | Samajwadi Party |
| TDP | – | Telugu Desam Party |
| TMC | – | Trinamool Congress |
| UP | – | Uttar Pradesh |